LIFE SKILLS GUIDE FOR TWEENS

Empowering Tools to Nurture Confident, Independent Preteens with Cooking, Money Smarts, Healthy Friendships, and Emotional IQ for a Happy, Fulfilling Life

Karen Cordoba

CONTENTS

Introduction   VII

Chapter 1.   Discovering The Super You   1
    Discovering The Super You
    Ready? Set? GROW!
    Self-Awareness
    Ready Player One
    Respawn
    Activity: Personal Skills Journal

Chapter 2.   Relationships   11
    Making and Keeping Great Friends
    Making Friends
    Keeping Friends
    Beyond Friends: Family and Mentors
    Activity: Friendship Challenge

Chapter 3.   Emotional Intelligence   21
    Understanding and Handling Feelings
    Emotions Unplugged
    Embrace Your Inner Emotion Hero
    Fighting Villains
    Activity: Emotion Diary

Chapter 4. School Life and Time Management 29

Navigating Your School Adventure

The Minefield of Middle School

Reporting for Duty

Prepare for Battle

Activity: Time Management Plan

Chapter 5. Personal Hygiene 39

Keeping Clean and Feeling Awesome

Body-Keeping

Renovations

Decorating

Activity: Hygiene Checklist

Chapter 6. Health and Wellness 47

Fuel Your Mind and Body

Taking Care of Your Instrument

Playing the Right Keys

Composing a Masterpiece

Activity: Recording Your Own Song

Chapter 7. Money Smarts 55

Learning to Be a Young Money Whiz

Make That Paper

Think Before You Buy

Budgeting

Banking

Activity: Budgeting Basics

Chapter 8. Cooking Skills 63

Fun in the Kitchen

Safety First

Embrace Your Inner Chef

Culinary Culture

Creative Cooking

Activity: Family Cook-Off

Chapter 9. Cleaning and Organization ... 71
    Tidying Up Your Personal Sanctuary
    Clearing the Clutter
    Clean Consistently
    Let's Organize
    Activity: Room Makeover Challenge

Chapter 10. Communication Skills ... 81
    Expressing Yourself and Making Lasting Connections
    What's Your Angle?
    How to Be a More Effective Communicator
    And the Academy Award Goes To...
    Talking Is More Than Just Words
    Activity: Silent Conversations

Chapter 11. Internet Safety ... 89
    How to Navigate Through Digital Challenges
    A Whole New (Digital) World
    Be Smart With Your Smartphone
    Activity: Digital Safety Plan

Chapter 12. First Aid ... 97
    How to Be Prepared in Case of Emergency
    Kitted Out
    Basic First Aid
    This is Not a Drill!
    Activity: Emergency Role-Play

Chapter 13. Leadership Skills ... 107
    Discovering the Leader in You
    Understanding Leadership
    Taking the Lead
    Teamwork Makes the Dream Work!
    Activity: Leadership Challenge

Chapter 14. Overcoming Life's Challenges ... 115
    How to Become a Problem Solver Genie

Facing and Overcoming Obstacles

Adaptability and Problem-Solving

Let's Solve It!

Activity: Challenge Journal

Chapter 15.   Setting Goals   123

Visualizing Your Future

Setting Your Coordinates

Chart Your Course

Stay the Course

Create a Map

Activity: Goal-Setting Workshop

Chapter 16.   Making Time for Fun   131

Life is a Beautiful Adventure

It's Not Just Playing

Finding Balance

It's the Little Things

Conclusion   137

References   140

INTRODUCTION

R eady for an awesome adventure? This isn't just any book: It's your passport to mastering some cool life skills. Buckle up, because we're about to dive into a world of fun and discovery, where learning life's big lessons is an adventure in itself!

Have you ever heard of IKEA? I mean, who hasn't, right? After all, it's one of the largest department store chains in the world! But did you know that the man who founded IKEA started out selling matches when he was just a kid? Yeah! From the age of five, he was knocking on the neighbors' doors, making moves! (*The Story of IKEA*, n.d.). Why am I telling you this? Because I want you to know that you don't need to wait until you're a grown-up to start something! Many of the wealthiest people in the world today started off learning how to sell things and handle money when they were the same age as you! We often look at grown-ups and think we'll wake up one day and just magically know how to do life, but that's not how it works at all. The person you want to become someday is counting on you to help them get there!

Would you like to know what you can do to help yourself succeed in the future? I'll tell you! You and I are about to go through a whole bunch of really important skills that will help you grow up to become the best version of yourself. You're probably going through so much right now that your head is spinning. Middle school can make you feel like you're stuck in the middle of nowhere. How do people even make friends? It's not like kindergarten where you could just offer the kid sitting next to you half your sandwich and boom!, you have a new best friend. People are getting so much trickier to figure out. And it's not just other people; you're changing, too. Sometimes it's like you don't even know who you are anymore or where you fit in. One week you're all about Taylor Swift and the next, you can't stand her.

Stuff you once gave the cold shoulder to are suddenly the absolute best thing since sliced bread. And what's the deal with braces anyway? Why are they even a thing? Your mom is probably on your case about cleaning your room all the time and doing your homework and you just wish she'd stop treating you like a kid when you're basically almost a teenager now. When will you ever catch a break? Trust me, I get it. Life can be a lot. But it doesn't have to be. Just take a deep breath. You've got this. I used to think I had skipped some secret growing-up class since it seemed like everyone else was just breezing through the very things that left me tossing and turning at night. It was like I was on a rollercoaster I didn't remember buying a ticket for. But do you wanna know a secret? You're not the only one who feels this way. Everyone is scared, and nobody has a clue. Some people are just better at pretending than other people. It's like people put a Snapchat filter on in real life and you're not really seeing who they really are. Behind all of that rizz is probably someone who's just as lost and confused as you.

I'm not gonna teach you how to pretend, though. I'm going to show you how to become the real deal! We're going to turn those filters into reality together. Life isn't all just an uphill battle, so try not to take yourself too seriously. Remember, you might not be a little kid anymore, but that doesn't mean you can't still have fun! Just go with the flow and see where life takes you. You're going to bump your head a couple of times, and that's cool. It just means you need to watch where you're walking. This journey can be as exciting or as terrifying as you choose to make it. So, let's make it an adventure. Let's laugh about your first zit and make fun of all the weird cringy things your body's doing. Let's talk about the tough stuff without making it awkward or turning it into a big deal. I'm going to level with you and tell you exactly like it is. Trust me, I've been there.

I'm sure you still have a lot of questions. Let's dig into them together. I'm not here to tell you how to live your life; I'm just here to make things a little less stressful and confusing. I low-key wish I had someone to show me the ropes when I was your age. I wish I had someone who could explain stuff to me that I was too embarrassed to ask my friends about. Things like why I suddenly need to wear deodorant or how to shave my legs. It's cool, I've got you. I know a thing or two about how to save up for that new PS5 game you've been eyeing when you know your parents aren't going to fork up the cash. I can also teach you a thing or two about taking care of yourself because there's no way you're going to survive the zombie apocalypse if the only thing you know how to make is grilled cheese.

Becoming a teen isn't as dramatic as you probably think. You just need to lock down the basics and everything else will be chill. Try not to sweat the small stuff, and don't be too scared to mess up. Everyone does it, and trust me, your friends aren't gonna bail on you just because your parents said you can't go to the Olivia Rodrigo concert. At the end of the day, being cool isn't as important as being yourself, so focus on that. Your life isn't going to end just because you don't have a million friends on Facebook. You don't need likes on your posts to feel good about yourself. Just like yourself, and that's enough.

I hope you learn some mad skills from this book. I hope you get the insider info you've been too scared to look up yourself. I hope, at the end of this, you're feeling a whole lot less stressed out about growing up. But most of all, I hope you have fun reading this. After all, what's the point of anything if you can't enjoy yourself, right?

1

DISCOVERING THE SUPER YOU

Don't go through life, grow through life.
- Eric Butterworth

When people talk about discovering yourself, you might get a little confused. I mean, what does that mean? Why do you need to be discovered? You've literally been right there all along! Sometimes, we think we know ourselves better than we actually do. Have you ever thought about how much you really know yourself? With all the changes you're going through while you grow up, you probably sometimes feel like a stranger to yourself. I used to just go along with all the stuff my friends were doing without really considering whether I actually liked it or not. You might be doing the same. It's like, well, if most kids your age are dressing a certain way or listening to a certain kind of music, you think you might as well do it, too. Maybe you even pretend to like it just for the sake of fitting in. But you can't really do that for the rest of your life. At some point, you should probably start trying to figure out some stuff for yourself. Like maybe you don't really like listening to Bella Poarch, now that you really think about it. Self-discovery is about taking a moment to really get to know yourself; like, the real you.

In this chapter, I'll be introducing you to yourself. I'm gonna show you how to shut out all that other stuff that you think you're supposed to be doing and start thinking of what you really want to do. You might find that you do legit like those things, and that's also cool. The point isn't about what you wear or who you hang out with. The point is to ask yourself if you're actually into those things or if you're just kinda going along with them. That's pretty much what self-discovery is all about. And then, when you're all clued up on that, we're going to kick it up a notch and look at ways you can continue improving yourself. Sound cool? Awesome, let's get into it!

Ready? Set? GROW!

Personal growth isn't about how many inches you grew taller over the summer, although that can be a pretty wild flex! Personal growth is about the stuff you learn that helps you become a better person.

Okay, so remember how you used to pick on your little sister all the time and make her cry? And now that you're older, you realize that maybe she's not so bad, and she's low-key pretty chill to hang out with sometimes? That's personal growth. It's pretty much what happens when you figure out or learn stuff that make you more mature than you were before.

And it's not just about how you treat other people; it can also be about the way you think and do stuff. Say you used to think doing homework was super lame, but now you've figured out that it's actually helping you learn. Yeah, that's personal growth, too!

Sometimes growing up is difficult, like when you realized it was time for you to stop playing with your Barbies. Or when you had to leave behind the school you loved because it was time for you to move on. We don't always like change; change can be scary. But, you know what? It's not a bad thing! When we let go of things, we make room for better things to come into our lives! Yeah, you probably missed your old school a ton. But after some time, you decided your new school was pretty awesome, too! We can't stay in the same place forever, as much as I know sometimes you wish you could. Growing up is exciting; you probably can't wait to be a teen and get to do so many amazing things and get some more freedom. But when that time comes, you'll also probably have to stop doing certain things. The awesome part is you'll probably know that you've outgrown them anyway and that better things are coming!

Think of it this way: Someday your favorite pair of jeans (you know, the ones you wear literally everywhere) aren't gonna fit anymore. You can try and force your legs into them, and you can keep wearing them even though they don't zip up anymore and the knees have holes. Or, you can find a new pair, a pair that you can learn to love just as much and won't rip every time you try to bend your legs. This is what growth means. It doesn't mean losing the things you love; it just means you accept that some things don't fit you anymore, and it's time to let them go.

Self-Awareness

Self-awareness is one of the most important skills you can learn. If you don't know what that means, just think of it as being aware of yourself. It's about knowing and understanding what your strengths, weaknesses, feelings, and values are, and also your dreams for the future. When you learn these things, you can make smarter choices and know how to act.

If you're confused about what strengths and weaknesses are, here's a tip: Your strengths are the things you're really good at and that you can do easily. Your weaknesses are tasks that are difficult for you and require extra effort. Have you ever thought about these things? If you haven't, now is a good time to start!

Get yourself a pen and paper and answer these questions:

- What are my five biggest strengths?

- What are my four biggest weaknesses?

- What are my three hopes for the future?

- What are two things I need to get better at doing?

- What's something I enjoy doing the most?

- What am I grateful for?

Ready Player One

Do you know what a mindset is? Let's talk gaming for a second. You know how when you start a game, you get to choose a character? You get a list of different characters, and you get to choose which one you want to play with based on what their skills are. Each character comes with a set level for their different skills, strengths, and weaknesses, and you kinda just choose the one you like best based on how you want to play the game. Then, there are other games where the characters are customizable. Sure, they also come with different levels of skills, but you can boost their skills by doing tasks and completing levels. Your mindset is pretty much the same thing.

Some people see themselves as a character born with specific skills and abilities with set levels. They think they must go through life doing things based on those skills, using their strengths to move forward and avoiding things they see as their weaknesses. When someone sees life this way, we say they have a fixed mindset. Other people see themselves as a customizable character, and they find opportunities to upgrade their skills and strengthen their weaknesses. These people have what we call a growth mindset.

The problem with having a fixed mindset is that it will stop you from trying new things for which you think you need to have the right skills. Say, for example, you're not doing so well at math. You'll just assume you're not good at math and give up. If you have a growth mindset, you'll see your math problem as a challenge you can beat if you try hard enough.

Having a fixed mindset can be tricky, especially when seeing others do well at things you need help with. You might see your friend get an A on a math test and get jealous because you wish you were born smarter. Someone with a growth mindset will go to their friend and ask them for help with math because they know that if they put the work in, they can become good at math, too!

Respawn

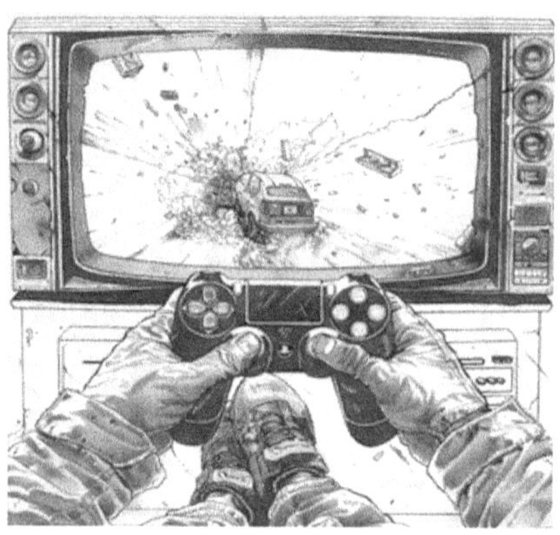

Since we're already talking about gaming, what happens when your character dies in the game? Is the game over? Do you delete it and try the next one? No, of course not! You respawn! You can do the same thing in real life; we call this resilience. Resilience is about not giving up when you fail at something or when something doesn't go the way you want it to. You get up and try again.

Unlike in games, resilience is more challenging than just dusting yourself off and picking up where you left off. It takes time, patience, and a whole lot of work. But what's important is that you try. When you're resilient, it doesn't mean you don't get hurt. Everyone gets hurt, and we all go through times when we're not feeling our best. Maybe a project you worked really hard on doesn't earn you the grade you thought you'd get. Maybe you stay up late studying for a test and still don't know all the correct answers. Maybe you didn't make it onto the soccer team this year despite training hard all summer. These things can all be pretty bleak and make you feel bad about yourself. But it's not the end of the world. If you beat yourself up every time you fail and tell yourself you're not good enough, you won't get anywhere. Don't get me wrong, you're allowed to be sad; that's normal. You're allowed to throw your game controller down on the couch in frustration. What you're not allowed to do is quit the game and stop trying.

When we're resilient, we don't let a little thing like failure keep us from reaching our dreams. You can look back, but only to remind yourself where you went wrong and figure out what you can do differently next time. Take your failures as lessons and carry them with you into your next attempt. Let's speak hypothetically for a moment: if you fall into a hole and can't escape, you should choose a different route next time. That's all failure is. It's an opportunity to learn from your mistakes and do better next time.

Do you want to be more resilient? Let's look at some things you can do to start learning how to respawn:

- Reach out: Talk to your friends and family about things that are upsetting you. Share your disappointments with them and get some advice. Maybe they've been through something like what you're dealing with, and they can help you cope. If anything, at least they can listen.

- Give yourself a break: Everybody makes mistakes, and nobody's perfect. Remember, you're only human, and it's okay to mess up sometimes. If you're going to beat yourself up, beat yourself up with a feather. Don't be so hard on yourself!

- Stay positive: Don't make mountains out of molehills. This means you don't need to make things out to be bigger than they are. Sometimes, we can turn the tiniest thing into the literal end of the world. Doing this makes it so much harder for ourselves to face the challenge and move on from it.

- Don't dwell: Speaking of moving on, make sure that you do! It's okay to sit in your feelings for a little bit, but don't build a house in them and call it home. When we spend too long sitting in pain and disappointment, we might get stuck there. Take the lesson and keep moving forward.

- Learn some coping skills: When you're dealing with challenges, try to figure out some things that help you feel better about your situation. These are called coping skills. It can be anything from journaling, painting, going for a walk, or talking to a friend. Coping skills are anything that gets you out of your head and back into the real world. Things you can do and use to help you feel better that are healthy and good for you! That last part is important. Screaming and breaking things is not a coping skill!

Do you enjoy takeout? Even if you don't, you've probably heard of KFC! Kentucky Fried Chicken is probably one of the biggest and most successful fast-food chains in the world! But here's a funny fact: The man who started it wasn't an instant success. In fact, Colonel Sanders was 62 when he finally convinced a restaurant to begin using his chicken recipe. Before that, he'd been rejected over a thousand times! (Breitegan, n.d.). Imagine he'd given up after the first or even one-hundredth rejection! Resilience isn't about trying until you're tired or trying until you've had enough. Resilience is about never giving up until you succeed! Think of that the next time you're eating your favorite dunked wings!

Activity: Personal Skills Journal

Create a journal to track your personal growth. Each day for a week, write down one new thing you've learned or a skill that you've practiced. Reflect on how these skills make you feel more confident and independent.

Let's recap what we've learned in this chapter:

- Personal growth is about learning things that will help you become a better person.

- Growing up is about letting go of things we've come to love to make room for better ones to come along.

- Self-awareness is about knowing and understanding who you are and what makes you tick.

- A growth mindset is the best way to help yourself become a better person.

- Resilience is what will help you bounce back from your failures and disappointments.

- Don't let failure stop you from trying again. Respawn!

2

RELATIONSHIPS

Friendship is the only cement that will ever hold the world together. – Woodrow Wilson

Making and Keeping Great Friends

L ife can be a great adventure, especially when you have people to learn and explore with you along the way. Friends are an important part of life because they are the people who you turn to when you're sad and laugh with when you're happy. Whether you have tons of friends or just two or three, everything is better when you have people you love around you. But how do you find your people? I know sometimes meeting new people and making new friends can seem nearly impossible, especially if you're shy and get super nervous around strangers. When I started high school, the scariest part was worrying about whether I would make any friends. I couldn't imagine how it would be having to eat lunch alone. How would I even know where to sit? I always wished I had a secret formula I could use to make friends or at least feel more comfortable meeting new people. Luckily for you, I found it! In this chapter, I'll be letting you in on the secret of how to be the social butterfly you've always dreamed of being.

Making Friends

Do you ever think back on the first time you met your best friend? You probably had no idea you were meeting someone who'd become such a big part of your life, right? The crazy thing about meeting new people is you never know where that one conversation will lead! And you never would have had that friend if one of you hadn't taken that first step to make a connection. The cool thing about school is that it allows you to practice hanging out with kids your age. Sometimes, striking up a random conversation is scary, but it gets easier with time.

Do you remember when you first had to learn how to ride a bike? It was so pretty tricky, right? I remember how much I struggled in the beginning. I thought I'd never get the hang of those pedals! But the more I practiced, the better I got. Soon, I could ride without even thinking about where to put my feet and how to use the handlebars. Riding a bike became as easy as breathing. Socializing can be the same way. At first, it can seem impossible, but with a little practice, you can start feeling super comfortable hanging out with people.

You're probably thinking, Okay, *but how do I actually talk to people?* I'm so glad you asked! Believe it or not, the best way to meet people is to go right up to them and introduce yourself! You really don't need to do anything fancy; just hop on over there and say hi. A lot of the time, the people you're too scared to introduce yourself to are just as nervous about socializing as you are!

I like starting off with a compliment just to break the ice, like going up to someone and telling them that I like their shoes. You should really like their shoes, though; don't just say something for the sake of starting up a conversation. You don't want a friendship that starts off on a lie! Once you've gotten all the awkward greetings out of the way, you can start getting to know them better. The best way to do this is by asking them questions about themselves.

You can try things like this:

- What's your favorite animal?

- What do you like to do for fun?

- Do you play any sports?

- Who's your favorite influencer?

Just ask them random stuff about themselves until you find something you both have in common; then, you can talk about that! Finding things you both enjoy is a great way to make friends with people who are similar to you. And make sure that you actually listen to what they have to say. Don't cut them off or try to talk over them; people don't like that.

I've had a few experiences with people who didn't quite get the hang of social skills, but one in particular really stands out. There was a girl in my class in middle school who was an absolute chatterbox. She literally talked a mile a minute and would jump from one topic to the next so fast it would make your head spin. She was super nice and super friendly, but nobody really wanted to be friends with her. Trying to talk to someone who never lets you get a word in and talks over you is not pleasant. She never understood why people didn't like her, mainly because she never stayed silent long enough to hear their explanations. As much as it's amazing to be comfortable talking to people, it's also important to be able to listen. Give others a chance to talk about things they enjoy and relate to your stories. Don't hog the spotlight!

Keeping Friends

Friendships are like flowers. You need to take care of them if you want them to stay healthy and keep growing. When we neglect plants, like forgetting to put them in the sun or not watering them for a few days, they wilt and die. Our friendships are the same. If you stop making an effort to be a good friend, you'll probably lose your friendships. If you want your friendships to last, be sure you make time for your friends and reach out to them. Making friends is just the first step; you also need to put energy into keeping those friendships going!

A good way to keep your friendships healthy is to ask yourself what you can do to make your friends happy. Try asking yourself these questions:

- When your friend is having a tough day, do you talk to them or try to cheer them up?

- When your friend does something great, do you tell them "Good job" or "Well done"?

- If your friend was worried about a test, do you ask them later how it went?

Sometimes, we get so caught up in our own stuff and focused on our own lives that we forget that other people have things going on, too. You never know; maybe that short message you send to someone offering support through a hard time is the one thing that makes them smile on that day!

Having friends isn't as important as having the right friends. I used to have a group of friends in middle school who did nothing but gossip about other people. It was pretty draining, and I didn't understand why I was so irked all the time. It turns out that being around their negative energy all the time was killing my vibe. I didn't like talking badly about other people for no reason, but I really liked having friends. In the end, I had to ask myself if it was really worth it to put up with their negative attitudes for the sake of having a group to sit with at lunch. Maybe you're in the same situation. Maybe you're wondering why you're putting up with friends who don't add value to your life. I decided I'd rather have no friends than bad friends, and I stopped hanging out with them. Sure, I was kinda lonely for a while, but eventually, I met some other people who I really connected with. I never would have met my new friends if I'd carried on hanging out with my old ones!

One of the things you'll need to learn how to deal with when it comes to friendships is having disagreements. I know it's not fun, but having small arguments with friends is something that happens. The key is learning how to handle these disagreements without hurting each other's feelings. Remember, fighting doesn't mean the friendship is over. You just need to communicate with your friends healthily and respectfully and work together to come up with a solution.

Tips to Handle Friendship Drama

Stay Calm

Getting worked up over things will make it more difficult for you to express yourself respectfully. Keep your emotions out of it when you're explaining your side and just stick with the facts.

Don't Cause a Scene

You really don't need to sell tickets to the show; this isn't a Netflix special. Keep the conversation private and talk to the person who upset you on your own. You really don't need to bring an audience; this will probably make things worse for both of you.

Think Before You Speak

Sometimes when we're mad, we say things that we don't mean. This can hurt people's feelings, and once the damage has been done, it may be hard to undo. Remember to think of what you're going to say before you say it. Imagine how the person hearing it might feel and try not to say things that will make them upset.

Own Your Part

This means you shouldn't only focus on what the other person did wrong to you. You should also consider what you did that made the situation worse and apologize if you need to. Pointing fingers isn't the best way to reach a fair agreement. If you both just own up and apologize, you can find peace a lot easier than trying to play the blame game.

Take A Breath

It's okay to leave a situation and return to it later once you've given yourself some time to think about it. In the heat of the moment, it isn't always easy to see things clearly, especially when emotions are getting in the way. Give yourself space to think through what happened in a relaxed way; you don't need to rush. Tell the person that you'd like a moment to gather your thoughts and give them that space as well. Maybe when you come back to it later, you'll see that you were both just making a whole lot of fuss about nothing!

Beyond Friends: Family and Mentors

Do you have people in your life that you look up to? I don't mean the celebs you follow on social media or the influencers you follow on YouTube. I mean people you know in real life who you respect and can go to for advice. As awesome as it can be to have people on social media that you look up to, having an adult in your life that you share a connection with and see as a role model is just as important.

Maybe you don't always want to ask your parents for advice, or you feel like they just don't understand you. Having a mentor can be super helpful in these situations because you can still get advice from a grown-up who probably knows a little bit more about life than you do! A mentor doesn't need to be someone in your family; it can be a teacher at your school or someone at your church. All a mentor does is guide you through life. They're the person you go to when you're confused about something or you're not quite sure how to handle a certain situation. They can be that one adult you feel comfortable asking embarrassing questions because you know they won't make fun of or judge you. Sure, you can always talk to your friends about things, but they usually only know as much as you do!

I never took French in school, but I had a French teacher as my mentor. She was really cool and easy to talk to, and she always gave me the best advice! I could ask her anything, from how to convince my parents to let me get a dog to what job I could someday see myself doing. She became like my second mother away from home, which was really great for me because my mother and I didn't have the best relationship at the time.

You might also have a grown-up in your life who kinda shows you where you're going wrong and whose opinion you know you can trust. The beautiful thing about having a mentor is that you never outgrow them. You'll probably have some kind of mentor throughout your life, guiding you along and helping you grow!

Activity: Friendship Challenge

Challenge yourself to make a new friend or strengthen an existing friendship. Plan an activity, start a conversation with someone new, or help a friend in need. Write about the experience.

Let's recap some of what we've learned in this chapter:

- Having friends makes life more exciting!

- Making friends is as easy as going up to someone and starting a conversation.

- Remember, the people you meet are probably just as nervous about socializing as you are, so take a leap of faith!

- If you want your friendships to last, you need to put effort into them.

- Learning how to deal with disagreements is an important part of keeping your friendships going.

- Find yourself a grown-up that you look up to and whose opinions you trust and get them to be your mentor.

- Mentors guide us through tough decisions and help us live our best lives!

3

EMOTIONAL INTELLIGENCE

Emotional intelligence is your ability to recognize and understand emotions in yourself and others, and your ability to use this awareness to manage your behavior and relationships. – Travis Bradberry

Understanding and Handling Feelings

Have you ever wondered how some people stay Zen all the time like they've cracked the code to eternal chill? Meanwhile, you're riding an emotional rollercoaster you never signed up for. Well, those people have mastered the art of emotional regulation. What's that, you ask? Buckle up: I'm about to spill the tea! Emotion regulation doesn't mean turning into an ice queen and feeling nothing. It means not letting emotions control you. It's not about becoming an emotionless robot but rather a master of your emotional world. Think of it like having a superpower! In this chapter, I'll show you how to unleash that power and become the emotion master.

Emotions Unplugged

First, let's understand those crazy creatures called emotions. If you're clueless about what you're feeling, how can you deal with it? Trust me, naming an emotion can work wonders! It's like putting a label on a package; it helps you make sense of things. And that's just the tip of the iceberg; we'll dive deep into emotional intelligence.

Unlocking Emotional Intelligence

Now, when you hear "intelligence," don't just picture nerds buried in books. IQ tests may measure academic smarts, but there's more to intelligence than acing exams. We've got musical intelligence, athletic intelligence, artistic intelligence, and even mechanical intelligence! One fascinating type is emotional intelligence, or EQ, for short. It's all about understanding, using, and managing emotions like a boss.

High EQ folks rock at navigating social and emotional situations. In a nutshell, if high IQ means book-smart, high EQ means people-smart.

But guess what? High EQ isn't just about handling your own emotions. It's a gamechanger for making better decisions, staying calm in tough situations, and building healthy relationships. Think about those viral TikToks of people losing their cool over the tiniest mishaps. Yup, that's a classic example of why emotional intelligence is a must-have skill. Nobody wants to be the star of a "meltdown moment" on the internet, right?

Emotion Name Game

Remember when I talked about naming your feelings? It's like giving them superhero identities! Once you know what you're up against, you can tackle it head-on. It's like describing your symptoms to a doctor. They won't prescribe the right cure if you can't explain what's going on. Don't leave your emotions shrouded in mystery; they deserve to be identified!

Think of your emotions as a way that your mind and body send messages to each other. If something is frightening you, your hands will get sweaty, your breathing will get superfast like you just ran a marathon, and your heart will start drumming out the beat to Taylor Swift's latest drop. This is how your body knows that you're on the verge of losing it, even if your mind still hasn't quite got the memo.

If you're not in the loop about what's going on, all of this can really freak you out, but that's not what your body's trying to do! Your body is just trying to let your mind know that it feels like you're in danger. Putting a name to that feeling and giving it attention is your mind's way of letting your body know that it knows what's up. However, without that, your body will keep getting more hyped up about it, and the feeling will get bigger and bigger as a way to get your attention. This is why ignoring your emotions can be so bad for you! It's like your body is spamming your brain's inbox and you're ghosting its messages. All you have to do is let your body know that you've received its message, and then it can relax. Don't bluetick your body's DMs!

Embrace Your Inner Emotion Hero

Now that we've laid the foundation, it's time to unleash your inner emotion hero! Get ready to put on your emotional cape and conquer the world. But first, let's dive into some practical strategies to help you harness your emotions like a pro.

Hit the Pause Button

Don't go through your day like someone hit fast forward on an episode of your life. Take a beat and think about how you're feeling. Notice even silly little things, like if you suddenly get super nervous when your teacher decides to hit you with one of those annoying surprise pop quizzes.

Emotional Bingo

Pick a feeling to pay attention to for the day. It can be any feeling that you think you get pretty often throughout your day. Make it your emotional buzzword for the day. Say your word for the day is "joy." Play "joy" bingo in your head all day. Every time you feel joy, just shout "bingo" in your head to yourself. It's a pretty fun way of keeping track of how often you feel a certain emotion and becoming more aware of the things that happen that can bring it up for you. Remember, get five bingo and you win a free toaster (not really)!

Feel It, Deal With It

Embrace the power of feeling and going through your emotions. Don't bottle them up or ignore them; they're here to teach you something. Acknowledge the emotion, give it a nod, and then figure out how to handle it. Remember, you're the boss, not your emotions.

The Thinking Game

Emotions can sometimes cloud our judgment, making it hard to make smarter choices. Enter the thinking game! Once you've acknowledged an emotion, take a step back and let your logical brain kick in. Look at the situation from different angles and make choices that make sense, not just those that feel good in the moment. For example, eating an entire tub of ice cream can seem like a good idea at first, but you'll probably regret it later!

Taming the Impulse Beast

Impulsive actions can get us into trouble, so it's time to tame the impulse beast. Pause before you react. Take a deep breath and give yourself a moment to think about the consequences of your actions. Think of it as giving a time-out to your impulsive behavior and giving your wise self a chance to shine.

Fighting Villains

So, you're ready to deal with your emotions, but what about those villainous ones that show up when you least expect them and threaten to overpower you? Yes, I'm talking about those pesky emotions like anger, fear, and sadness. I know, sometimes when you're experiencing difficult emotions, it can feel like they're your kryptonite. However, they don't always have to get the better of you!

The only way to prepare yourself for the battle is to practice. Waiting until you're in a situation to start learning new skills isn't always the best way to face your challenges with the confidence you'll need to overcome them. Equip yourself with the right defenses to defeat your opponents when the time comes. The best way to have the courage to face your difficult emotions when they come up is to teach yourself coping skills. When you know you already have all the weapons you'll need to defend yourself, you'll be less frightened when they eventually rear their ugly head. Next time you see a villain preparing to attack, raise your coping skills as a shield and protect yourself!

What are coping skills? Coping skills are little tricks you use to give yourself the space you need to not let your feelings get the best of you. It can be anything from taking a few deep breaths to going for a walk or to your happy place. Your happy place is an imaginary place you create in your mind where nothing can harm you. It can be whatever or wherever you want it to be and filled with things that bring you joy.

Another way to conquer your emotions is to find yourself an emotional outlet. An outlet is basically an activity you can do to redirect those feelings. Some good examples of emotional outlets are things like

- dancing,

- creating art, or

- writing in your journal.

So often, when we experience big emotions, we can feel like they're overpowering us. It's like they're too big to fit inside us, and we feel like we might explode! When you start feeling this way, you can always take all of that energy and direct it into something else. Using our emotions to create things like art can not only help you feel better, but you'll also have an awesome new art piece at the end as a reminder of your healthy effort!

The Ultimate Weapon

You know how every superhero has their own unique superpower? Well, in the world of emotional superheroes, the biggest superpower you can have is the ability to regulate your emotions! Some control minds, but you and I are going to learn how to control our emotions!

Emotional regulation is about being able to look at your emotions from a distance and decide how to deal with them. It's so much harder to handle something when you're in the middle of it. The feelings can cloud your vision and influence how you see and experience things. When you're able to take a step outside of the situation and see it from the outside, it becomes a lot easier. It's an incredible way to take your power back!

Activity: Emotion Diary

Keep an emotion diary for a week. Record different emotions experienced throughout the day and the situations that triggered them. Practice one relaxation technique and note its effect on your mood.

Let's recap what we've learned in this chapter:

- Emotional intelligence gives you the power to understand, use, and manage your emotions.

- Giving your feelings a name will make it easier to handle them.

- Emotions are how your brain and body send messages to each other.

- Learning coping skills will help you overcome difficult emotions.

- Emotional regulation is the ultimate superpower because it lets you deal with situations without letting your emotions get in the way!

Leave us a Review!

Loving the book so far? Drop us a cool review on Amazon! Your awesome thoughts could help other tweens rock their journey. Thanks for being a game-changer!"

Scan the QR code or visit the link. Thank you! (https://www.amazon.com/review/review-your-purch ases/?asin=B0D6BFRRL7).

4

SCHOOL LIFE AND TIME MANAGEMENT

Education is the passport to the future, for tomorrow belongs to those who prepare for it today. – Malcolm X

Navigating Your School Adventure

D o you often wake up dreading having to face another day of middle school? Sometimes going to school might feel like a warzone. You walk down the corridors with your books clutched to your chest like a shield because you have no idea where you should be going or what you should be doing. Learning doesn't need to feel like that; going to school can be a fun adventure, too! The only thing you should be fighting for is your future! Although, between you and I, sometimes math can really feel like a battlefield!

So, if you feel like you're behind enemy lines, let's work to get you back to home base where you feel safe. In this chapter, we'll be going through middle school boot camp. We'll be talking about all the skills you'll need to be able to be the best soldier ever!

The Minefield of Middle School

Moving from elementary school to middle school can feel like a huge adjustment, especially since you've just gotten used to being the biggest kid in school. It probably feels like you're starting from the bottom again, but it doesn't need to be that way. Remember how small you felt on the first day of elementary school? And it all worked out back then, right? The same will probably be true now!

Just take a deep breath and remember that change is a part of life. I know you wish you could just cover your face with mud and camouflage into the lockers, but it's not all that bad once you get used to it!

Another thing that might be making you nervous is having to move around for your different classes. It was so much easier when you knew you'd be in the same classroom all day and you knew exactly where your seat was. Now you need to find your way through busy halls full of so many people you don't know and still somehow make it to all your classes on time! Do yourself a favor and get a map! Check the school office or ask your teacher if there's a school map available that shows where classrooms are located. Make yourself familiar with the territory; it'll help you feel more at ease when you know the best route to all your classes.

And what about the social structure? Making it through that minefield alive can feel like a life-or-death challenge! Join the wrong crowd, sit at the wrong table, and boom!, your dreams of popularity will go up in smoke. Hey, don't stress, you'll find your way. Just be careful and watch your step. Make sure the people you're moving toward are the ones you can build meaningful connections with and don't just choose friends based on their social status.

To guide you on your mission, here are a few essentials to keep in your arsenal:

- Avoid combat: As much as we all want in on the action, protect the peace by not involving yourself in unnecessary drama. Middle school kids might be unkind, but you don't have to act the same way.

- Focus on the mission: It's so easy to get in with the wrong group of people who might want to pressure you into doing things that you know aren't okay. You're allowed to say no, even if it means you seem uncool.

- Respect your superiors: Much like in the army, the people in charge probably have a lot to teach you and a lot of great advice that will help you move forward. Pay attention to what they have to say. Your teachers are there to help you make the most of your schooling experience, so let them.

- Pick your battles: You're not going to get along with everyone, and not everyone is going to like you, but guess what? They don't have to! You can't go through life trying to please everyone. The only person you need to impress is yourself, so focus on that and don't sweat the rest.

Reporting for Duty

You're going to have a lot more going on in middle school than you did in elementary school. Sometimes, you might even feel like you're drowning or lost at sea. Learning to be organized and managing your time properly can be the life raft you need that leads you back to shore. I used to feel like I was being attacked from every direction sometimes. I had homework and assignments coming at me left and right and nowhere to run for cover! You might find yourself feeling that way too at some point. The best thing you can do is learn now how to deal with the pressure by tackling one thing at a time and giving yourself the room you need to do so.

Tackling Time

When you're faced with too many items on your itinerary, you might feel yourself starting to panic. How can you possibly do everything you need to do in a short period of time? Two words: time management. Time management is the skill of knowing how to use your time super effectively. A great way to help yourself manage your time is to create a to-do list. There are even apps you can download that will help you keep track of it. You should be able to review your to-do list and identify the most important things that need to be completed first. When you organize your tasks like this, you're less likely to forget to do something or run out of time before a deadline. Not everything you need to do needs to be done immediately. Focus on the things that are more pressing first, and don't spend too much time doing things that aren't urgent.

A good way to practice good time management skills is to make a daily schedule on the weekends. Plan out your day down to the hour if you need to. Make sure you have everything accounted for and that you've included everything in your daily planner that you need to get done. It can be so tempting to start with and dedicate more time to fun things than those you'd rather not do. Learning time management will help you resist this temptation because you'll be focusing on what's most important instead of what's the most fun! Not sure how to start? Let's look at an example you can use as a guideline:

Daily to-do list

- Morning (7:00 a.m. - 8:00 a.m.)

    - Wake up (7:00 a.m.)

    - Quick breakfast (7:30 a.m.)

    - Get ready for school (7:45 a.m.)

- School time (8:30 a.m. - 3:00 p.m.)

    - Attend classes

    - Participate and take notes

- After school (3:30 p.m. - 5:00 p.m.)

    ○ Snack and relax (3:30 p.m.)

    ○ Homework and study (4:00 p.m.)

- Evening (6:00 p.m. - 9:00 p.m.)

    ○ Dinner with family (6:00 p.m.)

    ○ Free time (7:00 p.m.)

    ○ Prepare for bed (8:30 p.m.)

    ○ Bedtime (9:00 p.m.)

Take a moment to think about how you spend your time. On a piece of paper, write down the things you dedicate most of your time to. Now, write down the most important things you need to get done. If these lists look different, now you'll understand why you struggle to get things done!

Prepare for Battle

One of the most important parts of learning at school is studying. Preparing for a big test can feel like you're getting ready to go to war. You might feel stressed, nervous, and anxious. When you feel unprepared for a quiz, you might get flustered! Having good study skills is the best way to combat these feelings!

Here are some ways you can help yourself build strong study skills:

- Prepare a place where you can study in a peaceful environment without distractions.

- Have your notes set out neatly.

- Set yourself goals.

- Remember to take regular breaks.

Sometimes, you can sit for an hour and feel like you haven't learned anything, and this is a sign that your study skills might not be up to scratch! It's not always about how much time you spend studying but rather how effectively you study that really makes the most significant difference.

Remove distractions from your study environment by doing things like

- turning off your phone.

- asking your family not to bother you during that time.

- not having things in the area that will draw your attention away from your books.

- asking a friend to study with you to help each other stay focused, even if you're not studying the same thing.

Taking breaks to give your brain time to reset will also help make your studying more effective. During your break, do something that will completely take your mind off studying, such as

- going for a walk.

- making yourself a snack.

- listening to some music.

Be Wise, Organize!

Don't you hate it when you're running around like a headless chicken looking for something you so desperately need? And why does it always happen when you're already running late?! The best way to beat the stress is to stay organized!

When everything has its own place, you'll always know where to find it! Keep your life in check by having specific spots where you put your things.

Good organization skills include:

- getting yourself ready for school every morning.

- packing your school bag.

- always putting things back where they belong when you're done using them.

- making to-do lists and checklists.

- breaking your tasks down into steps that are easy to follow.

Activity: Time Management Plan

Create a weekly planner. Include schoolwork, hobbies, and relaxation time. At the end of the week, reflect on how well you managed your time and what you could improve.

Let's debrief on what we've learned in this chapter:

- The battlefield of middle school doesn't need to be a warzone!

- Get the lay of the land by making yourself familiar with the territory and knowing the best route you can take to each of your classes.

- Make sure you have the right people on your squad; people you can trust to have your back.

- Prepare yourself for battle by learning how to manage your time and keep your space organized.

- Building good study habits will put you in the best position for success!

5

PERSONAL HYGIENE

Take care of your body, it's the only place
you have to live. – Jim Rohn

Keeping Clean and Feeling Awesome

Have you ever seen those TV shows where they fix up homes and thought, *Wow, those houses are so cool! I wish I could live there!* Or those shows where they clean up really messy houses and make them look like they're from a magazine? Think of your body as the house you live in. If you don't maintain and care for it properly, it can become rundown and start to show signs of neglect. But if you keep up with maintaining it and regularly clean it, you'll see yourself truly shine! Sometimes you just look at a house and know immediately that you could never go there because of how neglected it seems. You might stumble on all kinds of gross things in there! And then there are those houses you look at and just dream of living in because it's so pristine and well-kept. Well, people can be the same way. In this chapter, we'll be learning how to keep your body looking and feeling its best! So, what are you waiting for? Let's get started!

Body-Keeping

Much like a house, you need to regularly clean yourself if you want to keep your body healthy and sparkly. We call this personal hygiene. Personal hygiene is the daily habits you put into your routine that make sure your body is clean and healthy and keeps you feeling great! Having good personal hygiene will make you feel more confident and keep you from having to worry about whether you have bad breath or body odor.

Let's look at some of the most important personal hygiene habits you need to keep your body looking magazine-worthy.

Showering or Bathing Daily

Taking a bath or shower at least once a day is a good way to wash away any germs or bacteria that might have built up over the day. Make sure to wash your whole body and use soap. It's also a good idea to wash your hair once or twice a week. If you have oily hair, you might need to wash it more often than that.

Brushing Your Teeth Twice a Day

The best way to avoid bad breath and cavities is to make sure you brush your teeth twice a day. Be sure to brush for at least two minutes to get all of those germs out. It's also a good idea to floss and use mouthwash as well in case you missed something stuck between your teeth. Taking good care of your teeth will not only keep them bright and white, but will also help you avoid getting cavities!

Wearing Clean Clothes and Socks

I know you might want to wear your favorite pair of jeans every day, but it's important for you to wear clean clothes. Nobody wants you turning up to school with last night's spaghetti stained on your shirt!

Wearing a fresh set of clothes each day is the best way to know you're not smelling sweaty, and the same goes for socks. Wearing the same pair of socks over and over again can lead to stinky feet, and nobody wants that!

Trimming Your Nails

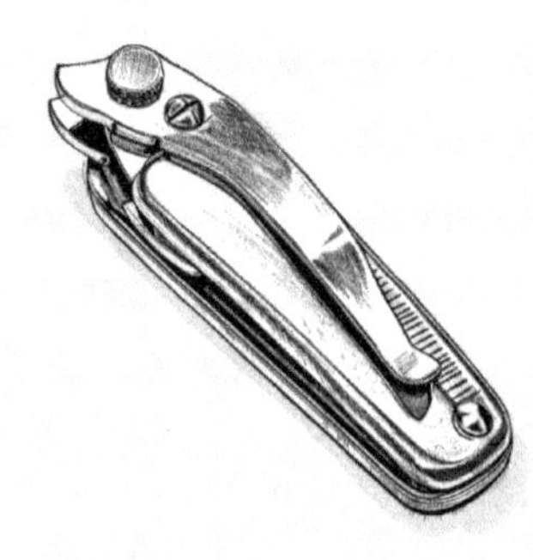

You'd be surprised how much dirt and bacteria hide underneath your fingernails! It's not always easy to see, like if you've been digging in the garden. The best way to keep your nails from becoming a free vacation for germs is to keep them trimmed and always remember to scrub them clean when you're bathing or showering.

Wash Your Hands

A good habit to get into is washing your hands as often as you can, especially before you eat, after using the restroom, or after you've been playing outside. We touch so many things throughout the day, and there's no telling what kinds of yucky germs we pick up along the way. The best way to protect yourself from getting sick is to make sure your hands are always clean!

Having good personal hygiene isn't just about keeping yourself clean and healthy or protecting yourself from getting sick. Good hygiene also helps your confidence. Just like those pretty houses we like looking at, making sure you're always looking and feeling your best will make you feel just as fabulous and picture-perfect!

Nobody wants to be in that house at the end of the street with the overgrown grass that nobody wants to visit. We all remember the one kid in class who had bad breath or always smelled kinda funny. Bad personal hygiene can make other kids not really want to hang out with you and might even lead to you being bullied or teased. Following these simple routines will keep you from having the same reputation as the haunted house on the block that everybody talks about but nobody actually wants to go near.

Renovations

As you prepare to enter your teen years, be prepared for some major renovations happening to your body! Some of these changes might confuse or scare you, but they don't need to; your body is just being upgraded! Teen years are the time when your body goes from that of a child to an adult. This happens in a number of ways, and some of them aren't fun.

Have you ever seen a house that's in the middle of being renovated? It looks like a hot mess! There are building materials and tools everywhere, rubble from walls being knocked down to make more room, and random paint samples on the walls. When you look at a house during this process, it's hard to imagine how the result might look because everything is so chaotic. You might feel a lot like this during this time of change, so don't be alarmed! The process of going through your body renovations is something we call puberty.

In simple terms, like I mentioned earlier, puberty is the time when your body starts to change from that of a child to that of an adult. Puberty can be a scary time because you're not sure what exactly is happening to your body. It's hard to see through all of that chaos, but trust me, you're gonna be okay! You might start experiencing some growth spurts and feel a little out of sorts for a while. Depending on your biological gender, you might start developing breasts or experience a change in your voice. And be ready to start sprouting hair all over! It also includes emotional changes and changes in how you interact with others. Remember that these changes are all a normal part of growing up, and everyone goes through them!

Puberty is like a super exciting body upgrade that happens to everyone during their teen years. For boys, it means shooting up in height, voices getting deeper, and hair sprouting in new places like the face, underarms, and around the private parts. They might also get stronger and start to sweat more. For girls, they'll also grow taller, their hips might get wider, and they'll start to develop breasts. Girls will also get hair under their arms and around their private parts, and they'll start having a monthly period, which is when the body gets ready for the possibility of having a baby in the future. Both boys and girls might notice more pimples and feel new, strong emotions. It's all a thrilling part of growing up, and it happens to everyone at their own pace.

If you're feeling alarmed, talk to a grown-up you trust about what you're experiencing and how it's making you feel. It's also important to remember that not everyone grows and changes the same way or at the same time. There's nothing wrong with you if you start seeing these changes earlier or later than your friends. Your body will develop at its own pace; it's not a competition! It's normal to feel a little odd over the next few years. Puberty can be difficult, especially if you're dealing with things like acne or feeling incredibly awkward after a growth spurt. Be patient with yourself and keep in mind that this isn't your final form. You're just a work in progress!

Decorating

The style and colors people use to decorate their houses can tell you a lot about them. Some people go with plain beige paints and standard lawns while others choose bolder colors and forest-like gardens. We make up our minds about what kinds of people live in the houses we see based on how they look. The same can be said of people.

The way you dress and make yourself up can tell people a lot about you as a person. Your style is a great way for you to express yourself as the beautiful, unique person that you are! What would people say about you if they looked at you? What ideas would they come up with about the kind of person you are? Have you ever thought about that? Take a second to think about whether the way you decorate yourself tells people the right story about you or if maybe it's time to do a little remodeling!

I know it can be so tempting to copy what your friends or favorite influencers are wearing, but you need to also remember to be true to yourself. Not every paint color suits every house! Make sure the style you choose to wear works with what you're working with! For example, if you don't feel comfortable wearing something, don't wear it anyway just because you saw Taylor Swift wearing it! She dresses in things that fit her body, and so should you! When I was in middle school, everyone started wearing platform sneakers. There was literally nowhere you could look without spotting at least five different pairs! I was pretty clumsy and could fall walking across a flat surface, so I already knew even attempting to wear anything with a platform was a recipe for disaster. Still, I decided to tempt fate for the sake of fitting in. It went about as well as you can imagine, and I didn't last a day in them before I'd twisted my ankle!

The pressure to fit in, especially when it comes to fashion, can sometimes feel so overwhelming that you just want to cave in. But remember that school isn't suburbia where everyone's lawn has to look exactly the same as their neighbors. Don't be scared to try new things with your hair or wear whatever you feel comfortable in. Who knows, you might just start a new trend!

Activity: Hygiene Checklist

Make a daily hygiene checklist including tasks like brushing your teeth, showering, and wearing clean clothes. Tick off each task for a week and note how it impacts your mood and confidence.

Let's unpack some of what we've learned in this chapter:

- Personal hygiene is like housekeeping!

- Make sure you include healthy hygiene habits in your daily routine to keep yourself healthy and clean.

- Good hygiene can help boost your confidence.

- Puberty is a time for big changes in your body and can feel awkward and confusing.

- Talk to an adult you trust about your challenges and experiences; it might help make the process easier for you.

- Remember that everyone goes through puberty at their own pace.

- Fashion is a great way for you to express yourself, so don't be scared to try new things!

6

HEALTH AND WELLNESS

The body is like a piano, and happiness is like music. It is needful to have the instrument in good order. – Henry Ward Beecher

Fuel Your Mind and Body

Health and wellness may seem like familiar topics that you've probably never dived into, but they hold the key to an exciting journey. When you're young, it's easy to overlook your health because your body usually feels fine. However, as you age, neglecting self-care will catch up with you. Imagine your health as a song, with your body as the instrument. The melody you create depends on how well you practice and care for your body. Just like two people playing the same song can produce different sounds, the quality of your health depends on the effort you invest and how well you maintain your body. Similarly, two people engaging in the same sport can have different levels of skill, influenced by their health maintenance and regular practice. In this chapter, we'll explore how to achieve a healthy and happy life by fine-tuning the elements necessary for the perfect symphony of health and wellness.

Taking Care of Your Instrument

One of the most important aspects of becoming a great musician is to take good care of your instruments. Have you ever heard someone play a song on a guitar that hasn't been tuned properly? You can hear that something is off; you just can't quite put your finger on what it is. The same can be said about your body. If you think of your body as being the instrument you use to play your music, then you can understand why it's so important for you to look after it.

You might not immediately feel the effects of not taking good care of your physical health, but you'll definitely notice that something is a bit off. The best way to take care of your body is to exercise regularly. Much like when you play an old piano and the keys sound dull and lifeless, not exercising can cause your body to become more tired, and you'll find yourself having less energy to do things.

When you exercise often, you not only keep your body feeling fit, but you're also helping yourself be healthier and less likely to get sick. Exercising will prevent you from getting diseases like obesity, diabetes, and heart disease when you get older. Exercise will keep your muscles and bones strong and give you the energy you need throughout the day.

Did you know that exercising can also help lift your mood? It's true! When you exercise, your brain releases chemicals, known as hormones, into your body. These specific hormones, called endorphins, are the hormones that tell your mind that you're happy!

Sometimes when we think of exercise, we picture people running laps around a track or lifting heavy weights at the gym. But the good news is that exercise can mean a lot of different things! It's not just about training or going to the gym; you can exercise doing just about anything. For example, if you love playing sports, that's definitely exercise! Even just running around in your backyard tossing a ball around with your dog counts as exercise!

If you're someone who doesn't really like formal kinds of exercise, find ways to include exercise in your life by doing things that you enjoy. Maybe go for a hike, jog through the park, or ride your bike around the block. There are so many creative ways to get physically active! Don't leave your instrument to gather dust up in the attic; get it out as often as you can and strum some mad tunes!

Playing the Right Keys

As important as it is to take care of your instrument and to practice playing, you also need to know what keys you're playing and how to

use the instrument to create the kind of music you like. In life, we can compare this to nutrition. The keys you need to play to create the sounds you want to hear is the same as knowing the right foods you need to eat to stay healthy! Everyone eats, and food is a pretty big part of your daily life. The thing is, *what* do you eat? Are you eating the right things for your health? Do you know the right keys to play to create the sound you want? Or are you just banging away, eating whatever you want, and hoping to somehow create a musical masterpiece?

When I was a kid, my parents bought me a mini piano. I used to love playing it and could sit there for hours. The only issue was that I had no idea how to read music, and I had no clue what I was doing, so I basically just sat there banging on the keys. As you can imagine, the music I created wasn't really anything that the neighbors were too happy to be hearing! Nobody becomes a musical genius by accident. It takes time, dedication, and patience. They need to be guided by the right people and given the right advice. The same can be said for your health. Getting it right isn't a matter of trial and error. You need to make sure you're doing the right things and eating the right foods if you want to get the results that you want.

Do you eat healthy food? Take a moment to think about the kinds of food you enjoy eating regularly. Write down five of your favorite foods. If it's all just snacks and candy, you're probably not following a healthy diet! It's perfectly okay to enjoy a bowl of ice cream every now and then, but you shouldn't be having one for dinner every night! Healthy eating isn't about eating bowls of steamed broccoli; it's just about making sure the food you eat has all the right vitamins and nutrients you need to keep you going through the day.

You can eat a lot of food and still not be healthy; that's because *what* you eat is more important than *how much* you eat. For example, one bowl of oatmeal in the morning is better than eating half a box of sugary cereal. Drinking water is also a pretty great way to stay healthy. A lot of people think that drinking fruit juice instead of soda is a healthy option, but there's actually a lot of sugar added to those fruit juices!

You don't need to start eating salads and nuts all day, but including at least one piece of fruit a day is definitely a good start! Let's look at some other nifty tips for healthy eating:

- Eat a lot of different foods instead of lots of the same thing.

- Instead of grabbing a candy bar for a snack, go for a piece of fruit.

- Never skip breakfast!

- Plan your meals to make them more exciting.

- Drink lots of fluids, especially if you've been exercising or if it's a hot day. Make sure you drink at least four to five glasses of water every day!

Looking for some healthy meal options? Try these:

- Grilled chicken with steamed vegetables

- Homemade turkey and veggie wrap

- Whole grain pasta with tomato sauce and a side salad

- Baked fish with quinoa and roasted sweet potatoes

- Oatmeal with fruit and nuts for breakfast

How can you plan your meals? Try using these easy steps:

1. Make a list of favorite foods and ingredients.

2. Choose a variety of foods from different food groups.

3. Plan meals that include fruits, vegetables, whole grains, and lean proteins.

4. Help with grocery shopping to pick up the items needed.

5. Get involved in cooking and preparing meals.

Composing a Masterpiece

All of the best composers could write out an entire symphony without ever touching an instrument. How did they do this? With their minds! Your mind is an incredibly powerful tool, and if you use it right, you can create the most beautiful melodies. Before you can pick up an instrument or learn what notes to play, you need to make sure the music you're creating in your mind is good.

This is why taking care of your mental health is as important as taking care of your physical health. When you're feeling low, you're probably not going to want to do anything physical. You'll feel tired all the time and won't have the energy to do any of the things you should be doing to keep yourself healthy, like eating nutritious meals. You'll end up eating comfort foods, like junk food and takeout. Everything starts with the mind, or the music you're creating. When you get your mind in the right space, other things will come much easier. You'll see things more positively and be more excited about making healthy choices to improve your life.

Have you ever heard of mindfulness? Mindfulness is a skill that involves being fully present or giving your full attention to where you are at that moment. It's about tuning out any distractions and just letting yourself be. When we're mindful, we can quiet down everything else that's happening outside of ourselves in the world around us and just focus on being where we are.

A good way to practice mindfulness is to just close your eyes and listen to the music of life. Hear the birds chirping outside your window, the neighbor mowing the lawn, the cars driving by, and the sounds of nature all around you. This beautiful natural symphony of life isn't something we often pause to appreciate. We're so busy living our own lives that these wonderful sounds have become just white noise in the background. When we take a moment to be quiet and listen, we can appreciate the part we play in the grand orchestra of the world and how these sounds color our lives and experiences.

Activity: Recording Your Own Song

Write down your food and activity for a week. Use a log to note what you eat and how much you move each day. Aim to include at least one new healthy food and physical activity.

Let's rewind and look at what we've learned in this chapter:

- Staying active through physical activity is one of the best ways to keep your body fit and healthy.

- Your body is your instrument, and you need to take care of it if you want the music you create to sound beautiful.

- Exercise doesn't need to be formal; it can be anything active that gets you moving and that you enjoy doing.

- Eating healthy gives you the energy you'll need throughout your day.

- What you eat is more important than how much you eat.

- Mindfulness will help you keep your mind in a good mental space.

- Take a moment to appreciate the natural symphony of life going on all around you!

7

MONEY SMARTS

Do not save what is left after spending, but spend what is left after saving. – Warren Buffett

Learning to Be a Young Money Whiz

You've probably come a long way from saving up money in your piggy bank for candy. You might think that someday when you're old enough to get a job and start earning a salary, then you'll learn about money, but that's not true! You're never too young to teach yourself the important skills you'll need to be able to manage your money properly. Any money you get—whether it's your monthly allowance or a gift for your birthday—is a great opportunity for you to start learning healthy financial habits and skills. Believe it or not, how you're going to handle money as a grown-up depends a lot on how you handle money now. This is because when you get into the habit of spending without thinking, it becomes a very difficult habit to break! In this chapter, we'll be talking all about money, learning fun ways to earn it, and smart ways to spend it.

Make That Paper

Is there an outfit you've had your eye on for quite some time, but your parents refuse to buy it for you? Is there a game you're dying to play, but your parents keep saying you need to wait until Christmas? You're probably wondering how you can earn some money to buy yourself the things you want. The good news is there are so many fun and creative ways that you can earn some money without having to get a part-time job! Let's look at a few ideas you can consider.

Chores

You might be surprised to find that the answer to your money problems is right under your nose! Offering to do extra chores around the house in exchange for money is a fun way to start practicing those business skills and also give your parents a break!

Remember, cleaning your own bedroom doesn't count! You can offer to do things like mow the lawn or clean out the garage and ask your parents if they'd be willing to pay you. If you think you've done a pretty good job, you can always offer the same services to your neighbors, too!

Babysitting/Pet Sitting

Offering up your services to babysit for families in your local community is a fun and engaging way to make some money. You can start by offering to babysit for people you know and slowly word of mouth will get around! You can also print some flyers and stick them up at the local supermarket or community center. Babysitting is a convenient side hustle because you can choose your hours and is especially great if you love kids!

Another service you can offer is pet sitting for people who are going on vacation. It mostly involves ensuring their fur babies have food and fresh water and maybe taking them for walks. This is a great way to give yourself something to do over the summer and earn a little extra pocket money.

Thrifting

Do you have an entire closet full of clothes but only wear, like, four outfits? Then thrifting might be a great idea! It has the benefit of helping you clear out that closet and also earning you some money at the same time.

Remember, something you've grown tired of wearing might be a dream come true to someone else. There are a few apps online where you can sell your clothes, or you can even go old-school and have a garage sale!

Selling Crafts

Are you nifty at making jewelry? Do you have a knack for creating personalized artwork? Why not cash in on those skills by selling your work? There's truly a market for everything these days, from knitted beanies to scented candles. Anything you can make can be sold. Remember to charge a fair price considering how much you spend on materials and the hours you put into making your items.

You can sell almost anything online using apps like Etsy. Or, you can look for a local market that you might be able to participate in.

Tutoring

Are you a math whiz? Why not channel some of that genius into your pocket? Tutoring offers you the chance to help out kids who might be struggling while helping yourself out at the same time! Teaching kids after school or over the weekends is a great way for you to earn a little extra money on the side.

Tutoring is great because you can offer both individual and group sessions.

Don't Forget to Save

You've probably heard your parents tell you a million times that money doesn't grow on trees, and it's true! As exciting as it is to earn money and think of all the things you can buy with it, you'll do yourself a lot of good if you start learning how to save. Saving money means that you don't need to spend every cent you have. You can put some away or even start a little fund so you can save up enough to buy something big.

When you learn to save money, you can take comfort in knowing that you don't need to ask your parents for every little thing you want, and you can spoil yourself every now and then.

A good way to start saving is to put away 10% or 20% of everything you earn, whether that's your allowance, or even money you've received as a gift. Getting into the habit of saving now will help you a lot when you're older and have a lot more responsibilities when it comes to money.

Think Before You Buy

When you have money, everything looks like a need. Suddenly there are all these things that you simply *must* have, whether you have any use for them or not. Your shoes could have been perfectly fine last week, but now that you have money, you just *have* to buy a new pair. I know that feeling; I used to be like that.

I hardly had time to put my money in my pocket before I'd already spent it. I had to learn the hard way that it doesn't matter how much money you earn if you don't know how to spend wisely.

Spending wisely doesn't mean pinching pennies and denying yourself anything fun. It just means that you think very carefully before you buy things and make sure that you're not just wasting money because you have it. A good way to decide whether something is worth buying is to ask yourself if it's a want or a need. A need is something that's necessary, like food, water, and clothing. These are all things you can't live without. Of course, the need for food doesn't mean you'll die without Dunkin' Donuts! A want is just something you'd like to have, like the latest pair of Air Jordans or the pair of jeans Billie Eilish wore in her latest music video. Wants are things you can live without but would really like to have. When you spend, you should focus on buying things you need first before buying the things you'd just like to have.

Budgeting

The best way to teach yourself how to save and spend your money wisely is to create a budget. A budget is a plan for how you're going to spend your money. When you already have a clear idea of the things you're going to spend your money on, you're less likely to waste money by using it on things you don't need or buying something on a whim.

For me, the best time to budget is *before* my money comes in! I've learned through experience that, as soon as that money is in my hand, my mind goes racing with all the things I could buy! I find it best to already have every dollar accounted for before I even have it and then I make sure that I stick to that budget. This doesn't mean I don't enjoy my money or buy myself nice things; it just means that I put a reasonable limit on how much I can spend on those things. When you budget, you can include things like going to the movies, going out for ice cream, or even just spoiling yourself with a new pair of shoes. As long as you've made room for those things in your budget and you're still managing to spend your money wisely, it's okay to get them. Having a budget will prevent you from walking past a store and seeing a pair of sneakers in the window and then dashing in to buy them before you've even given yourself a second to think!

Banking

In the old days, people used to put their money under their mattresses for safekeeping. Thankfully, we've come a long way since then! If you're unsure of your ability to hold onto your money and want to remove the temptation to spend it every time you see it in your wallet, you can always put it in the bank.

Banks are places where people put their money for safekeeping. You can even open up a savings account where you store your money until you're ready to spend it. Having a savings account is a great way to track your earnings and also how much you spend and what you're spending your money on. It's also a great way to keep track of how much money you have if you're saving up for something big.

Activity: Budgeting Basics

Create a simple budget. Include money earned from chores or allowance and plan how you'll spend, save, and share it. Track your spending for a month.

Let's add up everything we've learned in this chapter:

- Any money you receive is a great opportunity for you to practice healthy money habits and learn good financial skills.

- There are many fun and creative ways for you to earn an income, no matter your age!

- Saving a portion of everything you earn is an important skill to learn.

- Learn how to spend your money wisely, and don't get carried away buying things you don't need.

- Having a budget is a great way to keep track of your money, as well as your spending habits.

- Putting your money in the bank will help you resist the urge to splurge!

8

COOKING SKILLS

Cooking is at once child's play and adult joy. And cooking done with care is an act of love. – Craig Claiborne

Fun in the Kitchen

I f your parents were to leave you home alone for a weekend, would you be able to keep yourself fed? And I don't mean frozen dinners and takeout! If your answer is no, then you've got some work to do. Cooking isn't just a whole lot of fun; it's an important skill you'll need to learn if you want to be able to live on your own someday. You're probably so used to your parents having dinner ready on the table that you've never thought about the effort that goes into those amazing meals. In this chapter, we'll be strapping on our MasterChef aprons and getting down and dirty in the kitchen. Whether it's making yourself a quick sandwich or figuring out how to turn on the oven or air fryer, teaching yourself cooking skills is never a waste of time. So, let's dig in!

Safety First

Before we throw the meat on the grill, there are a few important safety tips you need to learn. Cooking is about more than just food; it's also about the experience of preparing the food. You need to make sure the food you cook is made in the cleanest, healthiest environment if you want your guests to return to your restaurant!

Here are some very important things to remember when working in the kitchen:

- Wash your hands: Before handling anything, make sure you've scrubbed your hands clean with soap and water. Nobody wants to taste the daisies you spent all afternoon planting in the backyard! Also, I know it's tempting, but don't lick your fingers while you're cooking either. You can taste that chocolate sauce later when you're enjoying your dessert!

- Keep your hair up: Have you ever found a hair in your food? It immediately ruins your appetite, no matter how tasty the meal is! So, make sure yours is safely tucked up in a hairband and out of your face and your pots.

- Use oven mitts when handling hot food: This includes any pots and pans you might need to remove from the stove. Anything that's spent any time under heat should be handled very carefully. Also, remember to always make sure that your pot and pan handles are facing away from the front of the stove. The last thing you need is to accidentally knock it over onto yourself. Ouch!

- Keep an eye on those knives: Knives used for cooking are normally very sharp and you can easily hurt yourself. If you're nervous, try practicing with a butterknife first, or ask one of your parents to handle anything to do with knives until you're more comfortable. Never throw a knife into a sink full of soapy water; someone might reach into it and hurt themselves. Always place knives facing down in the dishwasher.

- Follow the recipe: You're not Gordon Ramsey yet! Until you're more confident and able to cook a few basic meals, you'll probably need the guidance of someone who knows what they're doing. As exciting as it can be to just wing it, the last thing you want is to go to bed hungry after a failed experiment!

- Clean up when you're done: Try to leave the kitchen as neat as you find it. Make sure you've turned off all the appliances and wiped up any spills you may have made.

Embrace Your Inner Chef

Learning to cook is like learning any other skill. It might seem difficult at first, but with enough time, patience, and practice, you can become a culinary whiz!

To start with, try some basic recipes, ones that are quick and easy to make and don't need a lot of effort. Let's look at one fun idea you can try for each meal of the day to get you started on your journey!

Breakfast Parfait

Making a parfait is an easy way to make your breakfast look Instagram-worthy! It involves using the ingredients you'd normally include in your healthy breakfast, such as yogurt, granola, and fresh fruits, and building yourself a masterpiece!

All you need to make your very own breakfast beauty is to get a nice tall glass or a glass bowl (if you can't get glass ones, any bowl will do). Start by creating a nice layer of granola on the bottom, then add some fresh fruits on top of that.

Next, add a layer of yogurt. Repeat this until you reach the top of your container and voilà! Nice and easy! If you're feeling fancy, you can decorate the top with a dollop of whipped cream and some fresh fruit. And just like that, you'll have a healthy and appetizing breakfast to enjoy!

Pizza Bagels

These delicious treats are a great lunch option for those of you who love your pizza! It's also super easy to make and takes less than 15 minutes! All you'll need are some bagels, pizza sauce, mozzarella, cheddar cheese, and then any toppings you want!

First, you need to preheat your oven to 400 degrees Fahrenheit. If your bagels don't come precut, start by cutting the bagels in half (remember to be careful with those knives) and then spreading some pizza sauce on each half.

Next, put on as much cheese as your heart desires, and then finish it off with your toppings. When you're happy with your creation, put it into the oven and bake it between 5 to 10 minutes, depending on how gooey you like your cheese to be. Allow it to cool for a minute after you take it out of the oven and then chow down!

Grilled Cheese Sandwich

Who doesn't love a good grilled cheese sandwich? Imagine being able to have one whenever you want! Well, you can as soon as you've learned how to make it for yourself! Making grilled cheese is a lot easier than you think! It only has three ingredients: bread, cheese, and butter.

All you need to do is place a skillet on the stove and turn on the heat. If you're nervous about using the stove on your own, make sure you have a grown up there to help you. Next, butter a slice of bread and place it on the pan, buttered side facing down. Now, you can add your cheese to it. When you're happy with the amount of cheese, you can go ahead and put another buttered slice of bread on top, this time with the buttered side facing up. Cook the bottom slice until it turns golden and then flip the sandwich over. Keep flipping the sandwich until both sides are golden and the cheese is properly melted. And there you have it: Grilled cheese perfection for you to enjoy!

Now that you've got the hang of some of the basics, feel free to start exploring more recipes and expanding your skills! Who knows, you might just become the next Jamie Oliver!

Culinary Culture

One of the best things to learn is how to make those special dishes that remind you of your childhood. You know the ones I'm talking about; that one thing you can only eat if it's made by your mother. Food is such a wonderful thing because it connects people to their families through their culture. If you're from a specific ethnic background, like Mexican, Spanish, or Chinese, you'll probably have a few dishes that remind you of home.

I've always loved the way food can transport you to so many different places in the world! From the spices of India to the pasta of Italy, everywhere you go in the world people have their signature meals. Foods they prepare in a way that nobody else can. I'm sure you have a few of these in your family too! Why not ask your parents to show you how to prepare a few traditional family recipes? You can even look up some fun ones to try online! You don't need to travel the world to experience it. You can use your sense of taste to go to all the places you've always dreamed of visiting. And who knows, someday you might be able to go and enjoy those dishes there too!

Learning some of your traditional family recipes is a great way for you to not only bond with your family, but also to learn more about your heritage. When we share the recipes our family has passed down from one generation to the next, we honor the legacies left to us by our ancestors and also make sure that their stories aren't forgotten. Family recipes often come with exciting and interesting stories about our ancestors that we'd never have known otherwise!

Creative Cooking

When I was younger, my dad often made us pancakes on a Saturday morning. He would decorate them with blueberries and whipped cream that he'd always make into the shape of faces! We always had fun trying to guess what sort of face he'd be making that weekend. It was a fun family activity that we always looked forward to. These days, I've continued that tradition with my own children and love watching them play the same guessing game I always enjoyed as a child!

This story is a simple example of how fun cooking can be! It's not all about burning bacon and staying away from sharp objects. You can also make it a way to express yourself. Experimenting in the kitchen might just lead to you inventing something amazing!

As much as eating healthy is important, that doesn't mean that meals need to be a serious occasion. Turn your spaghetti into an octopus or your bacon and eggs into a face. Add feta to your watermelon just to see how it tastes (spoiler: It tastes amazing!). Learning how to cook can be as fun and exciting as you make it, so make the most of it!

Activity: Family Cook-Off

Choose a simple recipe from the book and cook it for your family. Note their feedback and how you felt during the cooking process. Share your experience and any improvements you made.

Let's recap some of what we can take away from this chapter:

- Cooking is an essential skill that you need to learn if you want to be able to take care of yourself.

- Kitchen safety is important both for the cleanliness of the food you prepare and also to avoid any nasty accidents while you're cooking.

- If you learn how to cook your favorite dishes, you can have them whenever you want!

- Cooking traditional recipes is a great way to bond with your family and learn more about your heritage.

- Find fun ways to express yourself creatively through food!

9

CLEANING AND ORGANIZATION

*Cleaning and organizing is a practice,
not a project.* – Meagan Francis

Tidying Up Your Personal Sanctuary

I *'m late for school and I can't find my books! Where did all my clean socks go? Oh no, I can't remember where I put my geography homework! Did I pack my gym bag already? Where are my sneakers?*

Does any of this sound familiar? This is what it sounded like in my head almost every morning before school. I could never find the things I needed when I needed them. I was always running late because I spent most mornings looking for lost items in places they had no business being! If you can relate to this struggle, then you—much like me—need to learn how to be organized.

I used to love living in the chaos. I felt like it gave my room character. I had no problem with the random clothes that littered my floor or the various books that were scattered across my study desk. I liked that my room looked *lived in.* No matter how much it drove my mother (and myself most mornings) crazy, I continued to live this way for years. I never liked my room being tidied up because I felt like it looked too clinical and stiff. To be honest, there were times when I would get to my wits end and spend an entire weekend cleaning and putting things away, making my room look perfect and tidy. Unfortunately, that would only last about a week until it returned to its natural state of chaos. As I got older, I started to see how much my disorganization was negatively affecting my life and decided it was time to change! Maybe you're feeling the same way, and I can definitely relate.

These days, I'm organized to the point of having labels on all my clothing drawers. It's been years since I went hunting for a clean pair of socks! In this chapter, we're gonna be learning how to leave those mad morning scrambles behind and keep your space—and sanity—in check.

Clearing the Clutter

Have you ever sat looking at a mountain of food and wondered how on earth you're supposed to eat all of it? Obviously, you can't shove it all in your mouth at once. You need to eat it one bite at a time. The same can be said for cleaning. Sometimes you can feel a little overwhelmed when you look at all the mess you have to clean up, but if you break it down into a bunch of smaller tasks, you'll find that it becomes a lot more manageable.

Cleaning skills are an important part of growing up; they'll help you when you're older and living on your own. Your parents aren't always going to be around to pick up after you, so you should probably start learning how to do things for yourself. Also, it's easier to know where your things are if you're the one who put them away! Here are some tips to help you not just clean your space but keep it clean.

Put It Back

These three simple words can change your life. You wouldn't believe how much time and effort you'll save if you put things back where they belong after you're done using them. If you're tired of having to look everywhere for your books or shoes, have a specific place where you keep them and make sure they're always there. Even if you're tempted to just kick your shoes off when you get home, take those few extra seconds to put them on the shoe rack. You'll thank yourself in the morning!

Tidy Up Before Bed

There's no better feeling than waking up to a clean room. It really makes me feel ready to get up and start the day. Tidying up before going to bed is also a nice, relaxing way to end the day. Set aside five minutes after you've done your homework to pack your books and set out the clothes you'll be wearing the next day. This will save you from the mad scramble in the morning to get all your things ready. You can just grab it and go!

Be Mindful

When you're getting undressed, make sure you put your clothes in the laundry basket and not just toss them on the ground. When you're done brushing your teeth, put the toothpaste back where it belongs. Being mindful of these small things can make a big difference to your space and keep it cleaner for longer.

Clean Consistently

When you live in chaos, there's bound to be those moments when you get a huge burst of energy and decide to tear through your room like a tornado, leaving cleanliness instead of destruction in your wake. Unfortunately, this isn't the best way to go about keeping your room clean. The best way to make sure that your room stays neat and tidy is to clean consistently.

This means that you do little bits every day instead of trying to do it all at once. This will also keep the mess from piling up to the point where you can barely move in there!

A good way to help yourself clean consistently is to create a daily or even weekly checklist of chores you need to do to keep your space clean. Your daily checklist can include basic things like making your bed, putting your dirty clothes in the laundry basket, and picking up anything you might have left on the floor. These are just small things you can do to keep your space looking neat and tidy.

For a weekly checklist, you might want to do a more thorough cleaning of your room. This can include things like

- emptying the garbage can.

- vacuuming the carpet.

- dusting your shelves.

- removing things that shouldn't be in your room like dirty dishes.

- folding away your clean clothes inside your drawers.

Doing these things weekly will prevent things from piling up. Nobody wants to deal with moldy month-old dishes!

Let's Organize

There's no point in cleaning if you're just going to mess it up again looking for that one sock that you can't remember putting away.

I used to go by the method of shoving things away wherever I could find space for them when I cleaned my room. This almost always backfired because I'd end up tearing my room apart looking for something!

The most important part of keeping a clean space is to organize it. Have specific places for things and make sure you keep them there. That means don't put your shirts in the sock drawer just because you're in a rush. When we organize our space, we create a more relaxing environment for ourselves.

It's so much easier to study at your desk when your books are neatly stacked on the shelf beside you. Being surrounded by mess can make it difficult for you to concentrate because you'll be distracted by the neon pink sock hanging from your lampshade! Learning to organize your room will help keep your life more organized. When you're in the habit of structure, it's easier to maintain a routine in other areas of your life. You'll learn how to manage your time better because you'll be getting into the habit of routine. It might seem like a small thing, but the skill of organization will have a big positive impact on your whole life.

You're probably wondering how you can start the process of becoming more organized. Here are some tips for you to apply to your daily life.

Create a Planner

How often do you forget about appointments or big tests? Events that are happening in the distant future can get lost in the endless stream of things you need to remember. You can help yourself by having a planner.

Buy a big calendar that you put up on your bedroom wall where you can fill in important events and assignments that you need to prepare for. You can even make the calendar yourself!

Make sure you check your planner often, so you know if you have something coming up soon. That way, you'll give yourself enough time to get ready for it.

Make Yourself Checklists

Start every day by writing out a list of everything you need to get done for that day, even on the weekends). When you know exactly what you need to spend time on, you're less likely to waste time on unimportant things. Tick off each item as you go along; this will give you a sense of accomplishment and show you how productively you've used your time for that day. Having a checklist also ensures that you don't forget to do important things.

Stick to Your Schedule

Don't just list what you need to get done. Assign yourself specific periods in which to get things done. Having a schedule is one of the best ways to teach yourself how to manage your time effectively. Set time limits on all your daily tasks. You can even assign yourself time for things like scrolling through social media or playing video games.

This is extremely helpful because you won't get sucked into wasting hours on your phone. You'll know that you have that time allocated to that, and that's it. This will also help you resist the temptation to constantly be going on your phone throughout the day when you're supposed to be doing other things.

Compartmentalize

Having things with compartments is one of the best ways to stay organized. This can relate to your backpack, your closet, and your drawers. Buying a backpack that has compartments to separate items is a good way to keep your bag from becoming cluttered and will make it easier for you to find the things you need. Compartments or dividers in your sock and underwear drawers will prevent this area from looking like a warzone too. Once you get into the habit of organizing things, you'll realize how much easier it makes your life and how much neater it makes your spaces!

Activity: Room Makeover Challenge

Organize and clean your room. Before and after the cleanup, take photos and compare. Reflect on how a tidy space affects your mood and productivity.

Let's unpack what we've learned in this chapter:

- When you keep your spaces clean, you make your life so much easier because you won't waste hours looking for things.

- Remember to put things back where they belong, tidy up before bed, and be mindful of how you take care of your spaces.

- It's worth the extra effort to return things to their places instead of just tossing them on the ground.

- Cleaning consistently is more effective than doing a massive cleanup when things get too messy.

- Getting organized will change your life!

10

COMMUNICATION SKILLS

Nothing in life is more important than the ability to communicate effectively. – Gerald R. Ford

Expressing Yourself and Making Lasting Connections

H ave you ever gotten frustrated with the characters on one of your favorite Netflix shows because of a misunderstanding? I get so worked up when I see my favorite on-screen couple about to break up because of a small misunderstanding. I feel like jumping into the screen and telling them to just listen to each other! And it's not just on TV; I've seen the same thing happen in real life. People argue over stuff without realizing they actually agree. You know what's similar about these situations? They show what happens when people can't communicate properly. Communication plays a huge role in our lives; it's involved in every interaction we have with others. As you can imagine, the inability to communicate can make your life very difficult. Sometimes what you're saying isn't the problem; it's how you're saying it, or how other people are comprehending it. In this chapter, we'll be exploring how you can learn to make yourself more effective at communicating so you can avoid starring in your own real-life Netflix drama!

What's Your Angle?

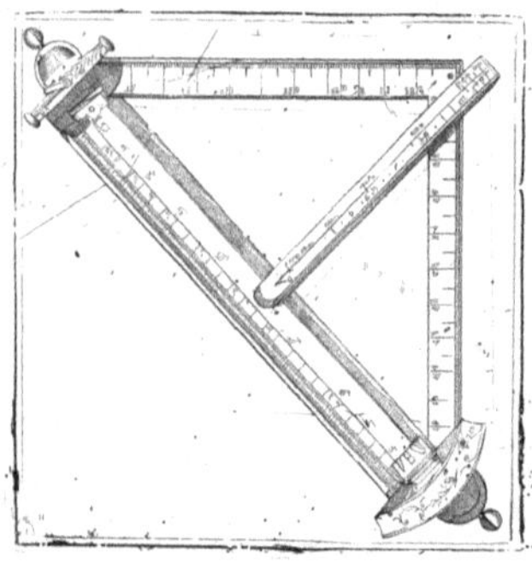

When it comes to communicating, everyone has their own way of doing it. People tend to fall into one of four different types of communication. See if you can figure out which one best describes you.

Passive

People who use passive communication are too nervous or afraid to speak their minds. They don't know how to ask for what they want or express their needs because they're afraid of hurting people's feelings or being rejected. passive people often put others before themselves.

Unfortunately, this causes them to end up being unhappy. They never express their own opinions because they're terrified of conflict, so they just end up going along with what other people say.

Aggressive

People who are aggressive communicators are the complete opposite of passive people. They only care about their wants and needs and don't really give anyone else a chance to speak their mind. They come across as intimidating, which makes people too afraid to stand up to them. They can even become confrontational when someone challenges them, resorting to name-calling, shouting, or anger to get their point across. As you can imagine, people who communicate aggressively are very difficult to get along with and impossible to reason with. It's their way or the highway.

Passive-Aggressive

Passive-aggressive people are just super sus. They might pretend to go along with what you're saying but secretly undermine you. They use things like sarcasm to tell people how they're really feeling. Have you ever been around someone who makes jokes about people that are personal and hurtful? Then you've probably met a passive-aggressive communicator. They'll never be upfront about their feelings, but they'll give you the silent treatment and expect you to know why they're upset. Dealing with someone who is passive-aggressive can be extremely frustrating because you're always playing guessing games with them about how they're feeling or why they're unhappy.

Assertive

Assertive communication is the best communication style. People who communicate assertively can express their wants and needs in an open, honest, and respectful way. They're also able to listen to other people's opinions and find ways to compromise to make everyone happy.

How to Be a More Effective Communicator

Be Understanding

Even if you don't agree with what the other person is saying, try to see things from their point of view. When we can learn to see things through other people's eyes, we can communicate our perspective with them better. Being understanding will also make it easier to respect other people's views and opinions.

Listen, Don't Just Hear

Sometimes when people are talking, we don't listen to what they're saying because we're too busy planning how we're going to respond. This can lead to unnecessary misunderstandings. Stop and listen to what the other person has to say. Take time to think about the point they're trying to get across before you respond. Ask them questions to make sure you've understood them correctly before continuing the discussion.

Meet in the Middle

Learning how to compromise can make communicating so much easier for you. Compromise doesn't mean you always agree with the other person and ignore your own feelings. Compromising means that you work together to come to a solution that works best for everyone. A win-win scenario.

And the Academy Award Goes To...

Being in social situations can be so nerve-racking and stressful. Sometimes you get tongue-tied and don't know how to approach a scenario or what to say. If you want to build up some confidence in your social skills, try doing roleplay! Roleplaying is when you find someone to act out different scenarios with you that you're feeling a little uncertain about. Practicing what to say or how to react in these situations will make it a lot easier for you when they come up in real life.

Here are some social situations where you can practice roleplaying:

- How to accept criticism.

- How to give someone a compliment.

- How to work in a group.

- How to introduce yourself to someone.

- How to ask if you can join in on a game.

- How to make plans with friends or invite someone over.

When you're acting out these scenarios, make sure you also practice how to respond to rejection. Being turned down can be hard, and in the moment, you might not know how to behave. Practicing how to take rejection with good grace will help you handle these situations with your chin up and your head held high!

Talking Is More Than Just Words

Communicating is about so much more than what you say. You might have noticed how, when people speak, their tone can show they're not really serious. That's because communicating includes not only your words, but also how your voice sounds and the facial expressions you're making too!

I know that sounds complicated, but it really isn't. For example, have you ever rolled your eyes at something someone has said? That's a way of communicating without words. And you know that look your best friend can give you from across the room and you immediately know you're both thinking the same thing? That's also communicating without words! Sometimes our facial expressions and body gestures can tell people so much more about how we're feeling than what we say.

Did you know that even the way you sit is a way of communicating? Crazy, right? When you're feeling upset and you sit with your arms and legs crossed, people probably know just by looking at you that you don't want to be bothered. When you rest your head in your hand and tap your fingers on the table, it likely shows your teacher that you're bored. There are so many little ways that we communicate with the world around us without even knowing.

Take a moment to think of examples of how we communicate without words. Write them down and then reflect on what your facial expressions and body gestures are telling people about you. When you become aware of how people are reading your facial expressions, you can learn how to be more effective in how you communicate with others!

Here are some helpful tips on how to use this to your advantage:

- Always make eye contact with people when you're talking to them. This shows the person that you're paying attention to them and that you're interested in what they have to say.

- Don't cross your arms and legs when someone's talking to you; it'll make them think you don't want to be there!

- Try to smile at people as often as you can; this will show them that you're friendly.

- Nod your head while people are speaking to show them that you're listening and agree with them.

- Avoid yawning or looking away while someone is talking to you, as it can seem rude.

- Tapping your foot or drumming your fingers while someone is talking to you can be seen as a sign of impatience, so try not to do that either!

- Don't make faces at people when they share something personal with you; you might cause them to feel offended or hurt their feelings.

Activity: Silent Conversations

Play a game with your friends where each one of you pulls a face or sits a certain way and the others have to guess what feeling they're expressing. It's a fun way to show each other how important it is to learn what you're saying to people without words. Afterward, journal about the experience and what you learned.

Speaking of learning, let's talk about what we've learned in this chapter:

- Learning how to communicate effectively is an important skill to avoid misunderstandings and miscommunication.

- Practice communicating assertively because it's the best style of communication.

- Being understanding, listening properly to what the other person has to say, and learning how to compromise are all ways to improve your communication skills.

- Roleplaying different social scenarios will help build your confidence when you're faced with those situations in real life.

- Communicating is more than just words. Learn how to read people's feelings through their facial expressions and body gestures.

11

INTERNET SAFETY

The internet gave us access to everything but it also gave everything access to us. – James Veitch

How to Navigate Through Digital Challenges

Everything is online these days; you don't even need to leave your house. You can buy groceries, check up on your friends, update your wardrobe, and pay your bills all at the click of a button. In minutes, you can have dinner delivered to your door. In seconds, you can connect to someone from across the world on a video call. The internet has made life so convenient, but it's also made life more dangerous. As much as there are many amazing things we can now do thanks to the internet, there are bad people out there who use this tool to cause harm to others. You must learn to protect yourself from these people and protect your information from people who might use it to hurt you.

Have you ever thought about internet safety? It's probably not something you think of often, even though we all use the internet almost daily. It's crazy to think it didn't even exist 50 years ago! Back then, you actually had to drive to the grocery store to get your food, and smartphones were unheard of. Now, they're so common your grandma probably has one (even though she barely knows how to use it!).

In this chapter, we'll be looking at all the things you need to do to protect yourself on the internet. Sometimes we forget that the internet has risks, and we might be too careless with what we share online. Remember, if you're not sure about something or feel uncomfortable with a certain situation, you can always reach out to a grown-up for help. You can never be too careful!

A Whole New (Digital) World

You were probably so excited the first time your parents let you explore the digital universe. So much to do, so much to see. You didn't spend a second thinking of all the potential dangers that lurk out there.

For most of us, the internet is an extension of our real lives, a place where we can stay connected with the people that we care about. Social media apps allow us to keep up to date with what's happening in the lives of the people who are important to us, especially those who live far away.

I've always loved that I can check in on old friends whenever I want. I get excited about celebrating their achievements from afar. In five minutes, I can literally catch up on 10 years of someone's life. I can know when they got married, when they had their first kid, and when they bought a new car, all without even having a conversation with them! You're probably looking forward to keeping track of all your friends after middle school once you've all gone to different high schools. Distance is no longer an obstacle to our friendships, thanks to the internet.

But there's another side to sharing our lives online, and it's the question of privacy. Just because you post about your life to keep your friends and family up to date, doesn't mean they're the only ones who will see it. I never gave a second thought to privacy settings on my posts when I first started using social media. I would post every little detail of my life down to what I had for breakfast. One day, I came across a story that rocked my world. It was about a girl who had been stalked online through her posts and then kidnapped. It really sent a shiver down my spine to see something so horrible. The internet has made it so much easier for people to reach you. An absolute stranger can know where you live, where you go to the gym, and where your favorite coffee shop is, and you wouldn't have a clue. This is why internet safety is so important. You need to be mindful of how much personal information you're putting online for people to find. You never know who might be scrolling through your profile.

Top Social Media Safety Tips

- Think before you post.

- Don't give people information that'll make you easy to find. Don't announce where you're going or tag the location of where you are, and especially don't post where you go to school!

- Don't talk to strangers. This is one of the most basic rules your parents taught you, and it applies in the digital world as well as the real world.

- Check the privacy settings on your posts, pictures, and videos. Make sure that only your friends can see them.

- Don't accept friend requests from people you don't know in real life. You never know who's really on the other side of that screen.

- Don't post anything you wouldn't want your parents to see. This means keeping your posts and photos appropriate. Imagine your future boss someday seeing them!

- Disable your location, especially when you post pictures.

- Trust your gut. If something doesn't feel right, it probably isn't. Talk to a grown-up; they can help you!

Be Smart With Your Smartphone

Being trusted with the freedom of having a smartphone means knowing how to use it responsibly. It's so easy to disappear into the online world and forget about the real world. I know because I've woken up many mornings with groggy eyes because I spent far too long watching videos on YouTube the night before.

You need to teach yourself how to use your phone responsibly. This means not letting the amount of time you spend on your phone negatively affect your daily life.

Building good digital habits will help you maintain a healthy life offline. Remember, the digital world is supposed to enhance your real world, not replace it. Let's take a moment to look at some ways to be smart with your smartphone.

Hold Yourself Accountable

- Limit how much time you spend glued to your screen. Never let your phone take away from the time you should be spending doing other things like homework, chores, or hanging out with your friends and family.

- Turn your phone off an hour before bedtime or put it on silent. You need to get at least 10 hours of sleep, and you won't get that if you're up late playing games on your phone or watching reels on Snapchat (*Sleep in Middle and High School Students*, 2020). Trust me, I should know!

- Put your phone away when you're doing activities with other people, like having dinner with your family. Sitting on your phone while people are trying to connect with you can come across as rude.

- Dedicate a specific amount of time daily that you spend on your phone and stick to it.

Use the Internet to Better Yourself

- Watch things that will help you grow as a person or teach you something about yourself and the world around you.

- Don't waste time on things that are meaningless and unnecessary.

- Follow people who inspire you to be better, not people who make you feel like you're not good enough.

- Don't compare yourself to the photoshopped images of celebs that you find online. They're not real!

- If you create content online, make sure that it paints you in a positive light. Don't use your feed as a personal journal where you vent about your life or rant about unimportant things.

Be Real

- Don't paint a picture of yourself online that isn't the real you.

- Avoid getting sucked into the mob when people say nasty or hurtful things about other people online.

- Stay true to yourself and your values, even in the digital world.

- You don't need to follow every internet trend or post things just for likes and attention.

Don't Succumb to Cyberbullying

- Don't give internet bullies attention; you're just giving them what they want.

- Block people who make you feel uncomfortable or say hurtful things to or about you online.

- Talk to a grown-up if you're being cyberbullied. Reach out; don't keep it to yourself.

- Don't fight fire with fire. You don't need to respond or react to cyberbullying.

Activity: Digital Safety Plan

Create your own digital safety plan. This plan can involve setting personal rules for internet use, outlining steps to take if you encounter online risks, and identifying trusted adults you can talk to about online experiences.

Let's download what we've learned in this chapter:

- Internet safety is about being aware of how the information you share online can expose you to potential risks.

- Check the privacy settings on your posts to make sure only your friends can see them.

- Don't talk to strangers online!

- Think before you post. Be careful of how the things you say might come back to you and don't share anything you wouldn't want your parents to see!

- Keep yourself safe by turning off your location before posting.

- Hold yourself accountable for how much time you spend on your phone.

- Use the internet to better yourself and improve your life.

- Be your authentic self online; don't pretend to be someone you're not.

- If you're being bullied online, reach out to a grown-up for help.

12

FIRST AID

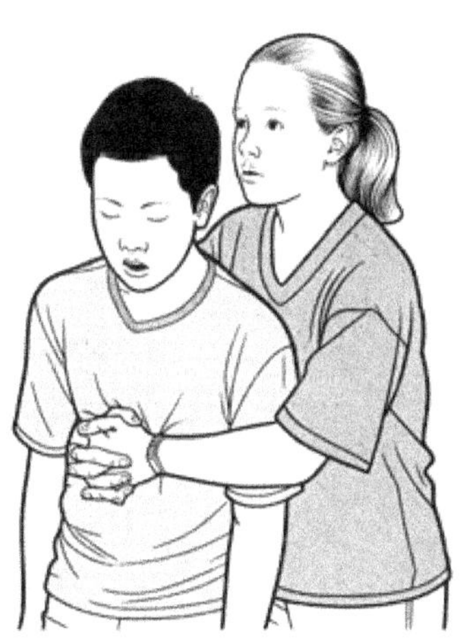

Take some time to learn first aid and CPR.
It saves lives, and it works. – Bobby Sherman

How to Be Prepared in Case of Emergency

H ave you ever seen a scene in a movie or TV show where someone starts choking? It's always so dramatic as someone calls out asking if there's a doctor in the room while another character—normally the hero—gets behind them and starts pushing on their stomach. Soon after, some unidentified object comes flying out of the choking person's mouth and they double over, gasping for air. Everyone breaks into applause as the person who was choking thanks the hero for saving their life. Choking in real life may not be as dramatic as in movies, but it's equally serious. The action they take to save the person choking in these episodes is actually a real form of first aid known as the Heimlich maneuver.

When it comes to real life, would you know what to do in case of a medical emergency? Are you familiar with the steps you need to take in case of an accident such as a bad fall or a burn? Having some basic knowledge of first aid can be pretty handy or, in extreme cases like the one we just described, lifesaving! Now, I'm not saying you're going to get a round of applause or a medal of honor, but you'll be a really great help both to yourself and the people around you. In this chapter, we're gonna dissect the basics of first aid and what you can do to help both yourself and others when faced with a medical emergency.

Kitted Out

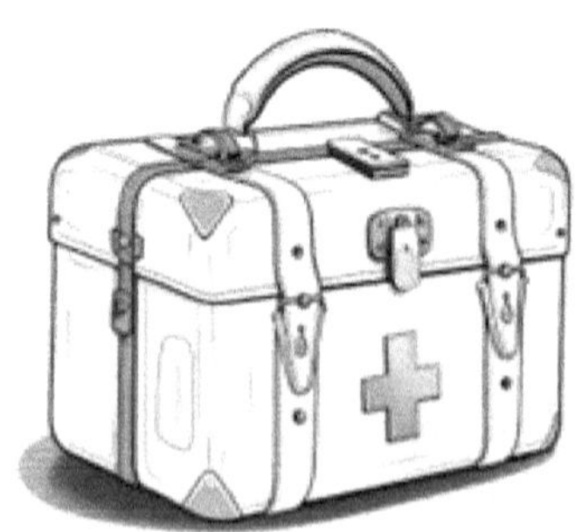

Do you know where your parents keep the first aid kit? If not, you should probably find out! Ideally, the first aid kit should be kept in a place where it's easy to get to in a pinch. You've probably seen a first aid kit before, but do you know what's in it and what all the items are used for? I won't lie, I used to have no idea how to use half the things in there! Aside from playing doctor as a kid, I'd never really taken the time to familiarize myself with the essential items used in household medical treatment. Lucky for you, we're going to unravel the mysteries of the first aid kit together!

Here are some of the most common things you'll find in a first aid kit and what they're used for:

- Manual: A first aid manual is a pretty important thing to include in a first aid kit. It contains emergency numbers you can call as well as some basic tips for how to handle medical emergencies and situations. Sometimes we forget what we need to do in the heat of the moment, so it's always handy to have one of these in there.

- Gloves: The gloves in the kit are there to protect the person using them from touching blood. If you're treating a wound, you should probably wear gloves. This isn't just to protect you, but also to keep germs on your hand from getting into the wound.

- Bandages or gauze: These are commonly available in rolls and are used to secure dressing (the covering that protects the wound to keep it clean) in place.

- Tape: These are used to hold dressings and bandages together.

- Scissors: For cutting gauze, tape, and dressings.

- Tweezers: These are used to remove splinters, stingers, and thorns.

- Antiseptic wipes/antiseptic solution: This is important for cleaning wounds and keeping bacteria out to prevent infection.

- Cold packs: These are used for sprains or bumps to help reduce swelling and ease pain.

- Thermometer: This is used to measure your temperature if you're feeling feverish.

- Ibuprofen: This is a pain reliever used to help you feel more comfortable after an injury or treat a headache from a cold.

- Cotton balls/cotton swabs: Used to apply antibacterial ointment onto injuries or to clean wounds. The ointment is that thick, oily stuff you spread over your wound to protect it from germs.

- Calamine lotion: This is used to treat any bites or stings from insects.

Looking at a first aid kit might feel intimidating because there are so many things, but once you know what they're all used for, you can understand the purpose of each in case of an emergency. Make sure to remind your parents to always keep your first aid kit at home fully stocked and to replace anything that might be running low. The last thing you need in an emergency situation is to realize that you've run out of gauze!

Basic First Aid

Going through life, you're bound to get a few scrapes and bruises. Knowing how to handle small injuries on your own is a pretty neat skill to learn so you're not running to your parents every time you bump your knee. Knowing a few basic first aid skills will also help you feel more independent and will definitely come in handy one day when you're living on your own. Obviously, you can't go rushing to the hospital for every scrape and bruise! You should learn how to take care of these little mishaps on your own. Let's look at some of the most common injuries you might deal with in your daily life and how best to manage them.

Cuts

If you fall and scrape or cut yourself in some way, the first thing you need to do is stop the bleeding. You can do this by applying pressure to the wound for a few minutes. Make sure you use a clean cloth or a towel to cover the wound; you don't want any germs getting in there! If the cut is bad enough that it hasn't stopped bleeding after a few minutes, you'll probably need to call for help.

Once the cut has stopped bleeding, clean the wound out with soap and water, an alcohol swab, or an antibacterial ointment. Be careful; it's probably going to sting a little, but that's normal. Let that dry for a minute and then you can go ahead and cover the wound up with a Band-Aid or gauze and a bandage, depending on its size and location.

Burns

A burn can happen in the blink of an eye, so be very careful around anything hot. When you get burned, your skin starts to cook, so your first step is to stop it from cooking! As much as you probably want to run for the nearest bucket of ice, that's a terrible idea. You might make it worse that way. What you need to do is run your burn under cool water, not too cold. Or you can get a clean, wet towel to hold over the burn. Never wrap anything tightly over a burn because the skin might get damaged. Instead, you can apply an antibiotic ointment to the burned area and then cover it with gauze or a bandage. If the burn is serious, you should probably go see a doctor.

Sprains

I used to be such a clumsy kid, and as a result, I twisted my ankle at least once a year. I was a professional at treating sprains by the time I was 12! If you're ever in a situation where you twist your ankle or sprain your wrist, don't put any pressure on it. Check to see if there are any bones sticking out or if it's twisted in an abnormal way. These are signs that you might have broken a bone, and you should get medical help immediately.

If it's just a sprain, you should get an ice pack, cover it in a cloth, and press it to the swollen part of your wrist or ankle for at least 20 minutes. This will help the swelling go down. If you don't have an ice pack, you can also fill a bathtub or bucket with cold water and give it a soak for that amount of time. Next, you can wrap the ankle in a bandage, being careful not to wrap it up too tightly. Make sure the bandage goes both around and underneath the affected area of the ankle to provide the right amount of support.

Bloody Nose

You've probably been told a million different ways to treat a bloody nose. When I was young, they used to tell us to throw our heads back and hold our noses, which was the worst! It always meant you'd end up swallowing blood and doctors have since learned that this is a very bad thing because it'll probably make you vomit. Yuck!

Instead, you should actually lean your head *forward* if your nose is bleeding. Hold a tissue with one hand to catch the blood and use two fingers on your other hand to pinch the bridge of your nose. That's the really bony part just above your nostrils. The bleeding should stop in about five minutes. If it doesn't, you should go see a doctor.

This is Not a Drill!

Do you know what to do if there's a serious medical emergency? The first thing you need to remember is not to panic. I know this is probably easier said than done, but if you remain calm, you'll probably be able to think more clearly and be more helpful.

One of the most important things you need to know is the number of your local emergency helpline. In America, this is 911, but you should ask your parents what the emergency number is where you're from. When calling for an emergency, you'll need to know your address and phone number, so make sure you have those memorized!

Here are a few important things to remember if you ever find yourself in an emergency situation:

- If you're on fire, you need to stop, drop and roll. This is to put out any fire on your clothes. If you're outdoors, grass is the best place to do this. If you're indoors, you should go for the tiles. You wouldn't want to accidentally set the carpets on fire.

- If someone has suffered a head or spinal injury, never move them. You risk causing more damage. Instead, try to keep their head and neck as stable as possible until help arrives.

- If someone is unconscious, gently tip their head back to make sure nothing is blocking their airway, and then check if they're breathing. You don't always need to touch someone to check if they're breathing. You can lay your head on their chest or watch to see if their chest is rising and falling.

How to Perform Cardiopulmonary Resuscitation

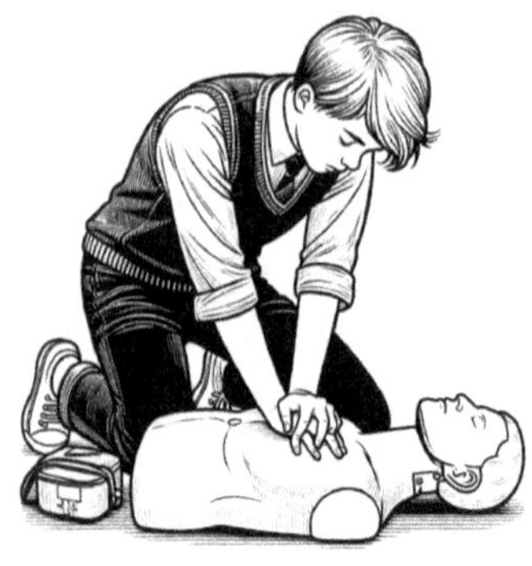

Cardiopulmonary resuscitation might sound like a mouthful, but it's just the official way of saying CPR. CPR is something you do in a situation where a person has stopped breathing or their heart has stopped beating. You would then perform CPR on that person to help them stay alive. CPR is done in three steps:

1. Chest compressions: Chest compressions are when you press down hard on a person's chest 30 times in a row. The point of this is to try and keep their blood pumping, so you're basically trying to get their heart beating again.

2. Check their airway: After doing 30 chest compressions, you should listen and look to see if the person is breathing on their own.

3. Rescue breathing: Rescue breathing is used to push air into the lungs of someone who isn't breathing. You need to close their nose and breathe air into their lungs.

You might find this process a bit much, but there's an easier way! A simpler way to perform CPR is by doing just the chest compressions. You can give the person a bunch of fast, hard chest compressions in a row. Aim for about 100-120 compressions per minute.

If you find yourself in a situation where you need to give someone CPR, make sure you've called for help while doing so. Keep performing CPR until help arrives.

If you're interested in getting certified to perform CPR, you can ask your parents to help you look online for CPR certifications in your area!

Activity: Emergency Role-Play

Practice what you would do in different emergency scenarios with family members or in a classroom setting. This will help you feel a lot more confident and prepared if you're ever faced with a real-life emergency situation.

Let's assess what we've learned in this chapter:

- You don't need to be a doctor to be able to be helpful in an emergency situation.

- Learning how to handle small mishaps and injuries will help you feel more independent.

- It's important to know when an injury requires medical attention.

- Memorize the emergency number for your local area.

- In the case of a fire: stop, drop, and roll!

- Know what's in a first aid kit and what each item is used for.

- CPR is performed to help someone whose heart has stopped beating and who isn't breathing on their own.

13

LEADERSHIP SKILLS

*A leader is one who knows the way, goes the way,
and shows the way.* – John C. Maxwell

Discovering the Leader in You

When you hear the word "leader," who is the first person that comes to mind? What about them makes them a great leader? We often look up to people for many reasons. It could be a president, a global icon, or a celebrity. No matter what role they play in the world, leaders all share similar traits that make people like and respect them. Leaders have a way of making people want to listen to them and hear what they have to say. They have a certain way of carrying themselves and interacting with people that makes them so influential.

Have you ever thought of yourself as being a leader? If not, why not? Much like everything else we've learned about so far, leadership is a skill. It's not just something you're born with; it's something you can learn to harness within yourself. In this chapter, we'll be focusing on what makes a person a good leader and learning how we can start to develop our own leadership qualities. Maybe someday, you'll be the leader that people look up to!

Understanding Leadership

What is a leader? Have you ever actually thought about that? A leader is someone with the ability to encourage and motivate others to achieve great things. It's not just about you being the best; it's about you being able to bring out the best in others as well. That's what makes a truly great leader.

Imagine being made a group leader for a math project and you're the only one in the group who passes. Does that make you a good leader? No! Being a good leader isn't just about your achievements and efforts.

It's about the impact you have on the people under your leadership. Being a leader isn't just about being in charge and bossing people around. It takes a lot of good people skills to be a good leader, and you can learn how to cultivate these skills in your everyday life.

You don't need to be a leader to have leadership skills either! Everyone starts somewhere, even presidents and influencers! Everyone has to start at the bottom and work their way up. Even if your goal isn't to become a global icon or a celebrity, learning good leadership skills will definitely benefit you in every aspect of your life.

Have you ever watched one of those speeches that put a lump in your throat? Like that moment in a movie where a sports team is sitting in the locker room at halftime and they're losing. The players have lost their spirit and look like they're about to lose hope. Then the coach comes in and gives a heartwarming speech that literally brings tears to your eyes and makes you wish you were out on that field. Usually, after the speech, the team goes on to win the game, despite the odds being against them. This is an example of being a good leader. Not just being able to give amazing pep talks (although that's definitely a plus) but being the person who can motivate others to keep pushing and not give up!

Qualities of a Great Leader

Confidence

You can't inspire people or get them to listen to you if you don't believe in yourself and what you're saying. Leaders often have to make difficult decisions and stand firm in them, and you need to be confident to do that. Being unsure of yourself or anxious in tense situations won't make it easy for people to believe in you. Leaders also need to stay calm in the face of conflict or hardships. Imagine the coach came into the locker room and became just as anxious and worried as the players. He'd never be able to motivate them to achieve!

Positivity

Being able to see the bright side of things is a great trait to have as a leader because you'll encourage the people around you to do the same. This doesn't mean you need to be a constant ray of sunshine, but choosing to be optimistic in every situation will definitely help lift people's spirits.

Effective Communication

Being able to communicate well with others is one of the most important skills that a leader needs to have. You need to be clear about your expectations of people and assertive in how you get your point across.

Empathy

Good leaders can connect with others and understand their perspectives and points of view. When people feel like you genuinely care about them and take their needs and concerns into consideration, it's easier for them to listen to and respect you. A good leader sees themselves as equal to others, not above them.

Resilience

A good leader doesn't give up when they hit an obstacle; they find a way to overcome it. Being resilient as a leader means you're the person who inspires others to not throw in the towel when things don't go as planned. You come up with a way to face challenges and not dwell on them or allow them to discourage you.

Taking the Lead

You don't need to wait for an opportunity to become a leader. You can take the initiative to be a leader in your everyday life. Leadership isn't a title, it's a mindset, and you can cultivate that mindset in everything you do, no matter how small. Here are some ways you can start taking the lead in your own life.

Be Helpful

Being a good leader means actively making a difference in the lives of the people around you. It means taking time out of your day to make someone else's a little better. Finding opportunities to help others no matter where you are is a great attitude to have in life. It doesn't have to be anything major either. They say charity begins at home, so why not offer to help your younger siblings with their homework to give your parents a break or clear the table after dinner without being asked?

If there's a local soup kitchen or charity organization you know of, you can offer your time up as a volunteer there. Being a part of your community and keeping in touch with how other people are living and the struggles they're facing are the hallmarks of a great leader. It'll teach you empathy and compassion as well as remind you to be grateful for all that you have.

Be a Good Role Model

To be a good leader, you need to lead by example. Very often, people don't listen to the words we say, but rather the way we act, to see what kind of person we are. It's so easy to do and say the right things, but your life needs to reflect those values and beliefs.

Being a good role model means making healthy choices, setting and achieving goals for yourself, and not succumbing to things like peer pressure. Live the kind of life that you'd want other people to follow. Be the kind of person you'd want other people to look up to.

Be Authentic

The best way to lead is to be yourself. Stand up for the things you believe in and live a life that aligns with your values and beliefs. They say if you don't stand for something, you'll fall for anything, and a good leader is someone who is able to stand firm in who they are and not be swayed by the ideas and opinions of others. If you want to be a leader, you need to be able to stand for what is right, even if you're standing alone.

Teamwork Makes the Dream Work!

One of the most important parts of being a leader is being able to work with a team. When you're the leader of a team, it's your responsibility to make sure that each member of the team is doing their part and that all of their contributions are acknowledged and appreciated. Being a team leader isn't just about handing out instructions to everyone on what to do and making sure that they do it. It's about listening to what everyone has to say and taking each of their opinions into consideration when it comes to making decisions. You need to balance each person's strengths and weaknesses and ensure that they're given tasks that fit those things. You also need to be able to motivate the group to try their best and set realistic goals that everyone can work towards achieving together.

Roles a Leader Plays in Teamwork

When it comes to completing a group project, a leader plays many important roles to ensure that the group goals are met. Let's take a look at some of them.

Appreciate Effort

A good team leader helps keep the members of their team motivated by celebrating their successes and appreciating their accomplishments. Nothing can be more disheartening than feeling like you've put all this work into something and nobody seems to notice. As a team leader, make sure you point out when someone's doing a good job and deserves a pat on the back!

Collaborate

As a leader, you should allow everyone on the team to participate in brainstorming ideas and sharing their opinions. People work better when they know that their input is being heard and that they're a valued part of the group effort. Don't just force your ideas and opinions on the group and expect everyone to go along with it. Allow everyone to do their part.

Be Empathetic

You must show that you care about your team members and their well-being. Check in on them from time to time to make sure everyone knows what's going on and understands the role they need to play. Be understanding if someone is struggling a little and offer them the support they need to get back on track with the rest of the team.

Set Group Goals

As important as it is for each person in the group to play their part and make sure that they do their best, it's also important to keep an eye on the bigger picture. As the team leader, it's up to you to set group goals and make sure that each person is making an effort to carry their weight.

Activity: Leadership Challenge

Take on a small leadership role in an upcoming activity or project and journal your experiences. Focus on what you've learned about leadership and teamwork.

Let's take a look at what we've learned in this chapter:

- Think about the qualities you think make a good leader and recognize ways you can start to learn the skills to become those things.

- Being a leader isn't just about being in charge and telling people what to do.

- A good leader is able to inspire and motivate others to achieve more and accomplish their goals.

- Confidence, resilience, positivity, empathy, and good communication skills are all traits of a good leader.

- When it comes to teamwork, a good leader is able to make each member of the team feel valued and appreciated for their efforts.

14

Overcoming Life's Challenges

*The greatest glory in living lies not in never falling,
but in rising every time we fall. – Nelson Mandela*

How to Become a Problem Solver Genie

Do you ever hear those heartbreaking stories about people who've had to overcome devastating circumstances and wonder how they did it? I've always found reading and listening to stories like that so inspiring. Stories about people who never gave up even though they faced immense challenges. I like these stories not just because they remind me to be grateful for what I have, but also because they show me how powerful the human spirit can be, like our ability to find the tiniest flicker of light in the darkest tunnel and follow it with everything we've got. I used to look at those people and think they can't be normal. They must have something inside themselves that the rest of us don't. The truth is that all of us have the strength within ourselves to overcome our challenges and triumph over our obstacles. The secret is to just never give up, no matter how many times you fail. In this chapter, we're gonna unlock that same powerful spirit inside of you and show you how to harness its magic.

Facing and Overcoming Obstacles

Middle school is hard, right? Trust me, I know. Things that were once so simple, like playing at recess, have suddenly become so complicated. Now there are cliques, and people care more about gossiping than eating their lunch. You're different, too. You used to be quite happy living in your own world and now you find yourself caring a little too much about what other people think. The tween years can be difficult for a number of reasons. Your body is changing in weird and wonderful ways that you can't control and sometimes you feel like a stranger in your own skin. On top of that, you're starting to notice things about yourself that never bothered you before, like that little extra weight around your waist that you wish would just disappear.

All of these things you're experiencing are normal, although they might feel the furthest thing from that. The first step to not allowing them to get the best of you is to not try and run away from them or pretend they don't exist. Accept that there are things that are making you uncomfortable and start thinking of ways you can manage these emotions. You can't overcome your challenges unless you're first willing to face them.

Common Challenges in Middle School

Bullying

Now that everyone suddenly cares what everyone else thinks about them, there are bound to be a few bad eggs. Bullying happens when people think that putting someone else down will make them feel better about themselves. Other people jump on the bandwagon because they're afraid they'll be next if they don't participate. It becomes very toxic very quickly, and being caught up in this vicious cycle can be really traumatic. If you or someone you're close to is being bullied at school, don't keep it to yourself. Don't put a brave face on at home and pretend like everything's fine. Talk to someone, even if it's one of your teachers.

Nobody has a right to make you feel unwelcome or unsafe at school or anywhere else for that matter. I know standing up for yourself sounds terrifying, but doing nothing is worse. Standing up for yourself doesn't mean fighting back; it means speaking up and letting someone know what's going on so they can help you. People don't have to like or accept you, but that doesn't give them the right to treat you badly.

Academic Pressure

As someone who used to cruise through school, middle school was truly a wake-up call for me. For the first time, I found myself actually having to study for tests! I wasn't getting the grades I was used to anymore and it was upsetting. I never realized until then how much of my self-esteem and self-confidence came from my achievements until I didn't have them anymore. Maybe you're feeling the same way. Maybe you're starting to question if you were ever even smart at all! The pressure to get good grades affects us all differently. Some people don't care, some people become perfectionists, and others are so afraid to fail that they don't even try.

What you need to remember is that, at the end of the day, it's not about what grades you get but about how much effort and dedication you put into your work. When you put your all into a project and the end result is something you feel proud of, that's better than any grade you can receive. Focus on appreciating your effort instead of your accomplishments. It matters that you tried.

Body Image

Chances are, you didn't spent much time thinking about your body's appearance before. Sure, you knew if you were taller or shorter than other people, or you liked the curls in your hair. But your appearance was never the center of your universe when you were younger. Now that you're getting older, you can't help but notice all the little things that make you different from others. Maybe your friends are getting their breasts and you're still flat as a surfboard. Or maybe all the guys in your class are starting to sound like Batman but you still sound like a chipmunk. The media doesn't help either. Everywhere you look, there are photoshopped images of flawless people being shoved in your face. People you wish you could look like but know you never will.

The worst thing you can do for your self-esteem is compare yourself to other people; worse still, people who have been edited! The people you're trying to look like don't exist. Learn to celebrate the things about yourself that are different because those are the things that make you unique!

The Power to Overcome

Overcoming challenges isn't easy, but it's possible. Facing them is one thing, and even that can feel a bit overwhelming sometimes. Let's look at a few tips for how you can start to overcome challenging situations in your life:

- Identify the challenge and brainstorm strategies for how to deal with it.

- Journal your thoughts and feelings and how this issue is affecting you.

- Reach out to someone you trust to talk about the problem and ask them to help you come up with solutions.

- Read up about experiences from people who've faced a similar situation and how they managed to overcome it.

Adaptability and Problem-Solving

Do you know what it means to be adaptable? Being adaptable means you can go with the flow of life and handle situations when things don't go the way you thought they would. It's almost like how a chameleon is able to change to suit its environment. You can be that way, too. When you're adaptable, coping with changes becomes less of a stress and more of an adventure! In life, change is inevitable. You'll be a lot happier if you learn how to deal with it instead of always going against the tide.

Being adaptable can benefit you in every aspect of your life. Say you're doing a project and it's not going the way you want it to. You can either get frustrated and angry, or you can switch it up and find a new way to go about it. Imagine how much time and effort you'll save if you learn how to adapt! Do you know how many of the world's greatest inventions were discovered by accident? People who set out to do something and, when it didn't go their way, adapted to the change and ended up having an incredible breakthrough!

We all had a big lesson in adaptability during the coronavirus pandemic. We had to suddenly learn how to reduce our busy lives to the confines of our homes. Some people really struggled to adapt to these changes and became miserable as a result. Others saw this as an opportunity to explore new interests and learn new ways of doing things and flourished as a result!

Learn How to Be More Adaptable

- Switch things up: Routine is great and healthy, but it can also make you a bit set in your ways. Every now and then, try switching things up! If you eat granola every day for breakfast, try something else for a week. Sit in a different spot at church than the same bench you've sat in since you were five. Small changes like this can bring you out of the monotony of your everyday life and teach you how to accept change.

- Try new things: Try out for a sport you've never played before or start a new hobby. Take up gardening for no other reason than to try it out. It's fun to do the things we enjoy, and it's even more fun to do the things we're good at. But when you stay in your comfort zone, you don't grow or learn to adapt.

- Change your mindset: Instead of seeing change as scary and unavoidable, get excited for the opportunity it presents. When things change, so do you. You get a chance to learn new things about yourself and explore new possibilities. Start seeing the positive side!

Let's Solve It!

One of the most important skills to have when it comes to overcoming obstacles and dealing with change is knowing how to solve problems. Adapting is about knowing where to go now that your original plan hasn't worked out. When you're confident in your ability to solve problems, unexpected changes will be far less scary or frustrating. You'll be able to more calmly deal with the new circumstances and find a way to move forward.

Here are six simple steps you can use to help you with problem-solving:

1. Identify the problem.

2. Identify what's causing the problem.

3. Come up with at least five different solutions you can use to fix the problem.

4. Evaluate the pros and cons of each solution.

5. Choose the best solution, then put it into action.

6. Reflect on the outcome of your problem-solving.

If the solution you tried doesn't work, you can always just go back and try a different one. The great thing about reflecting on the outcome is that you learn from your mistakes and have a better understanding of what you need to do the next time!

Activity: Challenge Journal

Journal about a recent challenge that you faced, how you dealt with it, and what you learned. Explore how you might approach similar challenges in the future.

Let's recap what we've learned in this chapter:

- You have the power within yourself to overcome your obstacles and face your challenges. You just need to unlock it!

- You won't overcome your challenges unless you're willing to face them.

- Standing up for yourself is about taking your power back and not letting the bullies win.

- Do your best at everything; that's what really counts!

- Being able to adapt to changes will keep unexpected events from overwhelming you.

- Learning how to solve problems will give you the confidence to face challenges.

15

SETTING GOALS

*The future belongs to those who believe in
the beauty of their dreams. – Eleanor Roosevelt*

Visualizing Your Future

Picture yourself five years from now, 10 years from now, 15 years from now. Where do you see yourself? What sort of person do you want to become? What kind of life do you want to live? We all have dreams and aspirations for the future, no matter at which stage of life we might find ourselves. Sure, they might change with time, experience, and maturity. Maybe when you were younger you wanted to be a pilot but now that you're older, you've realized you have a fear of heights! The older you get, the better you get to know yourself. It's probably a lot easier to picture a realistic future for yourself now than it was when you were younger. You've seen more of life, and you've learned what really matters to you. As much as we all have dreams, not everyone knows how to make those dreams a reality.

Do you wanna know a little secret? The best way to get to your dreams is to draw yourself a map that will take you there. The difference between a dream and a goal is a plan of action, a decision to put the effort into making those dreams a reality for yourself. In this chapter, we'll be learning how you can create a map that'll take you to where you want to be!

Setting Your Coordinates

Imagine you're about to go on a trip. You excitedly pack your things already dreaming of all the adventures you're going to have. You hop into the backseat of the car, and your parents ask you where you're headed, but you're not sure. Doesn't that sound silly? Going through life without goals is the same way. You need to put a destination into your GPS if you want it to give you directions! If you don't know where you're going, you'll never learn how to get there. This is why it's important to have goals.

Goals give your life a sense of purpose and direction and help you stay motivated to keep putting your best effort into things. When you know that everything you're doing is helping you get one step closer to where you need to be, you start doing things with greater care and more determination than before. Take homework, for example. I used to just scribble a bunch of stuff down for the sake of getting it out the way and over with and because I didn't want to get into trouble the next day at school. Then, in middle school, our math teacher came up with a great plan to have a competition. Every week, she ran a little raffle for a prize one of the students could win. Every time you got all of the answers correct on your homework, you'd get your name put into the hat. So, the better you did at your homework, the more entries you could have, and the greater your chances of winning. I've never been so focused while doing math homework in my life! The lesson I learned was that when you have a good motivation for doing something, you're more likely to put more effort into it.

When you give yourself goals like wanting to be the top student in your class or wanting to win a prize, you'll probably find that you put a lot more time and attention into doing your homework. Without an added incentive, you probably don't really see the point.

Having goals also helps you stay focused. You're probably not going to fall prey to peer pressure or give in to unhealthy distractions. For example, if your goal is to win at the swim meet that weekend, you're not gonna want to stay up all night talking to your friends on the phone the night before. Goals help you see the bigger picture and give meaning to the smaller choices you make throughout the day that might negatively impact your desired outcome. When you have a destination set in your internal GPS, you're not going to get lost or take a longer route to get there!

Chart Your Course

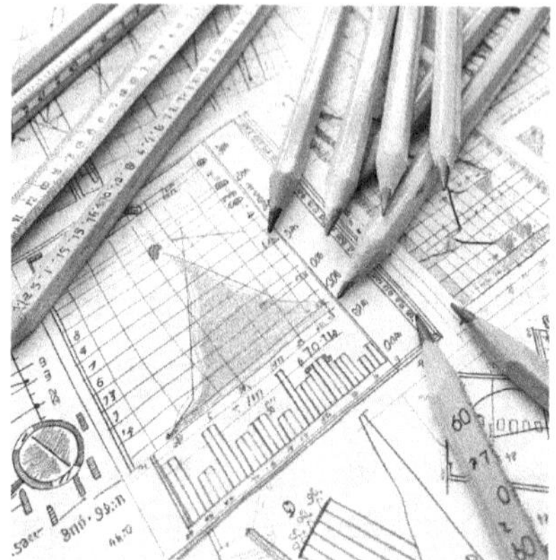

Now that we understand the importance of having goals, let's discuss how to set them. The best way to set goals is through the SMART method, and no, I don't just mean that it's clever! SMART is an acronym for goal setting. Let's break it down and see what it means.

S: Specific

The first step to setting yourself a goal is to make it specific. This means your goal must be clear and detailed. Having a vague goal will make it difficult for you to visualize it. For example, just saying, "I want to do well in school" is not enough. Make your goals more specific, such as assigning specific grades you want to achieve in each subject.

M: Measurable

You need to be able to measure your goal so you can track your progress. If you can't measure a goal, how will you know if you've achieved it? For example, saying you want to read more is not measurable. Instead, set yourself a goal to read three books this year. Not only is this goal measurable, but you'll be able to set yourself little milestones to celebrate your progress along the way. This will help keep you motivated.

A: Attainable

Setting yourself an attainable goal is important because you need to be realistic. When you create a goal for yourself that isn't realistic, you're just setting yourself up for failure and disappointment. Telling yourself that you're going to be the best tennis player in your school when you've never even held a racket is not an attainable goal. Make sure the goals that you set for yourself are within your reach and realistically possible for you to achieve.

R: Relevant

Make sure that the goals you're setting for yourself are beneficial for the future you want, will help you grow as a person, and serve some kind of purpose. Wanting to break the world record for collecting the most bottle caps is not a relevant goal. It's not going to make you a better person and it doesn't reflect your values or morals. Like, yeah, it's cool, but is it really worth the time and effort you'd be putting into it?

T: Time Bound

Setting a time limit for your goals prevents procrastination and maintains motivation for consistent progress. If there's no time limit on something, there's no sense of urgency for you to do it, and you'll probably end up putting it off indefinitely. Deciding that you're going to learn how to ride a bike is cool, but give yourself a time frame. Tell yourself that you're going to ride like a pro within three months and then work hard to make that happen!

Stay the Course

Life is unpredictable. As much as you can plan ahead, you're bound to hit a few speed bumps along the way. When this happens, it's normal to feel a little disheartened and wonder if your goals are worth pursuing. We've spoken about overcoming obstacles and facing challenges, but that doesn't make it easy.

When we fall, sometimes we want to stay down there and feel sorry for ourselves. But the best thing you can do is to get up, dust yourself off, and keep trying. Having a goal that means something to you is the best way to keep yourself motivated. When you have that end goal in mind, the little setbacks along the way are less likely to derail you. You've gotta keep your eyes on the prize!

Reminding yourself why you started in the first place can be helpful when facing these challenges. Look back on how far you've come and celebrate the little accomplishments you've already made along your journey. Picture what it'll be like when you eventually reach your goal and how all these minor setbacks will ultimately be worth it. Failure is hard, but remember that everyone fails. What's important is that you don't give up on your goals just because the road to get there isn't easy. If it was easy, everyone would do it!

Create a Map

One of the best ways to make your goals real is to create a visual representation of all the things you want to achieve. Have you ever heard of a vision board? A vision board is a map of the future you want. You can put pictures on it representing all of the things you want to achieve. Having this visual aid for your goals will help bring them to life for you.

Every time you feel like giving up, you can look at your vision board and picture yourself having everything you're working so hard for. A vision board is a great way to take your dreams out of your head and put them in the real world, somewhere you can look at them whenever you need that extra boost of motivation.

Creating a vision board can be a fun, creative activity to spend an afternoon doing! You can get a bunch of magazines out and cut out any pictures that inspire or motivate you. There might be phrases or quotes you find in there that you feel are uplifting; cut those out too! If you're looking for more specific things, you can print pictures off the internet. A good place to go for inspiring quotes and pictures is sites like Pinterest. Organize and arrange these images onto a board or large piece of cardboard. Make it as bold and eye-catching as you want, and make it represent everything you want and hope to achieve. When you look at it, it should make you feel happy, determined, and empowered. When you're done, put it up somewhere where you'll see it as often as possible, like on your bedroom wall!

If you'd rather not have a physical version, you can also create a digital version on your phone using images you find online. But make sure you look at it as often as possible. It might even be a great idea to make it your phone wallpaper!

Activity: Goal-Setting Workshop

Identify a goal and outline the steps you need to take to achieve it. Start your own vision board as a visual representation of your goal.

Let's look back on what we've learned in this chapter:

- The best way to achieve your dreams is to create a map for yourself on how to get there. You can do this by setting yourself goals.

- Goals give your life purpose and direction and motivate you to always do your best.

- Set yourself goals that are specific, measurable, attainable, relevant, and timebound.

- Don't give up on your goals just because the journey is rough. If it was easy, everyone would do it!

- Create a vision board to help you visualize your goals and make them real.

16

MAKING TIME FOR FUN

We don't stop playing because we grow old; we grow old because we stop playing. – George Bernard Shaw

Life is a Beautiful Adventure

I used to be such a jokester as a child. I was always finding ways to make people laugh and looking for the lighter side of things. If there's one thing I'm glad I've never lost as I've gotten older, it's my ability to enjoy life! You're entering a time in your life where people are going to expect you to be more mature, but that doesn't mean you need to be serious all the time. I always wished I never had to grow up because all the adults around me seemed so uptight. I was afraid that growing up meant I wouldn't get to have fun anymore, but I'm so glad that's not true. This chapter is a reminder to have fun! You're still young and you have your whole life ahead of you. Life is a rollercoaster, so strap in and enjoy the ride!

It's Not Just Playing

When you're having fun with your friends, you might not realize that these activities are actually improving your mental health and brain development. There are so many benefits to playing that aren't just about getting rid of all that excess energy!

Benefits of Playing

Brain Development

Believe it or not, when you're creating fun imaginary scenarios and acting them out with your friends, your brain is actually developing! This is because your brain is learning how to build connections between things, and you're also improving your problem-solving skills. A lot of the things you might not understand that happen in real life become clearer when you're acting them out in pretend scenarios with your friends. You can process things that have happened in a fun way or learn new ways to think about them. All of this is a great way to help your brain grow!

Physical Development

It's obvious that when you're playing, you're getting lots of exercise. But you're also improving your motor skills and strengthening your muscles and bones. Physical activities are also a great way to improve your reflexes and balance, too.

Social Development

Participating in activities with other kids is a great way to improve your social skills in an open environment. When you're all playing a game together, you're also building connections while having fun. You chat and laugh together, and it's a more relaxed way to get to meet new people and make new friends.

Mental Health

Playing is a great way to relax and forget about other things going on in your life that might be stressing you out. You can release any tension you might be feeling and it's a great way to de-stress. Being active also releases happy hormones into your body which means you'll feel more positive afterwards.

Finding Balance

One of the unavoidable parts of getting older is having more responsibilities. You don't get to goof around all the time; people have expectations of you and there are things you need to do. As a result, maybe you find that you don't get as much time to yourself as you'd like, or you don't play as often as you used to.

Finding balance is an important skill to learn as you grow up. Believe it or not, the responsibilities will just keep piling on, and it's up to you to manage your time to make sure you still get opportunities to do the things you enjoy. Have you ever heard the saying, "All work no play makes Jimmy a dull boy?" Well, it's true. If all you do is work without rest or taking time to unwind and let your hair down, you'll end up feeling miserable.

When planning your day or weekly schedule, be sure to allocate time for play. While scheduling it may seem less enjoyable, neglecting to do so could result in never finding time for it!

Finding Joy in Everyday Life

You've probably come a long way from running up and down in a cape pretending to be a superhero, but that doesn't mean you stop having fun! Play is still important as you get older; it might just look a little different now. Maybe these days your idea of fun isn't 10 hours of tag in the backyard, but you can still discover new ways of enjoying yourself.

Do you have any hobbies or interests? Taking time out to appreciate those things still counts as play. Taking a step back from life to spend time doing things that fill us with joy isn't something we lose with time. Find a passion and dedicate yourself to exploring it. It can be anything: hiking, rock climbing, scrapbooking, baking. Anything that makes you feel like a kid again and fills you with childlike wonder!

Now is a good time to start exploring hobbies if you haven't found one yet. Experiment with various activities until you discover the right fit. Sometimes we end up finding passion in something we never dreamed we'd like! The only way to know for sure is to try everything at least once. The worst thing that could happen is that you don't like it. Then you just try something else. Exploring a variety of different hobbies is also a great way to broaden your horizons and open yourself up to new experiences. You might even find a real purpose in a field you'd never looked twice at before! Hobbies are also an amazing way to remind yourself that there's so much more to life and the world than just school. We get so wrapped up in our books and so stressed about deadlines that life begins to pass us by.

It's the Little Things

Remember not to get so caught up in the big picture that you miss out on the little moments throughout your day that can make you smile. Be present in your life, be where your feet are. Take the time to value the people in your life who are important to you, and make sure they know how much you appreciate them.

Turn off your phone during family meals and actually have a conversation with your family. Catch up on what's happening in their lives, take an interest in things that mean a lot to them. When's the last time you went out into the backyard and played fetch with your dog? And I don't mean absentmindedly with one hand while your eyes were glued to your phone.

Do something to make someone else smile just because. Go for a long walk and appreciate nature. Lie under the stars at night and marvel at the wonders of the galaxy. Read that book you've had sitting on your bookshelf for ages. Find time to do things that mean something to you, things that matter. That's how you enjoy life: by living it.

Let's reflect on what we've learned in this chapter:

- Growing up doesn't mean you need to be serious all the time.

- Playing is important for your mental, physical, social, and emotional development.

- Finding balance between work and play is important for your well-being.

- Take time out for yourself to do things that you enjoy and that make you happy.

- Explore new hobbies and find your passion.

- Be present in your life and enjoy the little things.

CONCLUSION

Welcome to the grand finale of our journey! The skills we've uncovered in this book will set the stage for an awesome life if you put them into action. Success isn't just about knowing the right thing to do; it's about using that knowledge to your advantage. It's not luck; it's about patience, hard work, and maybe just the right amount of rizz! We've covered so much in this book, and there's so much knowledge for you to find. Before I leave you, though, let's look back on some of the most fundamental lessons you can remember going forward.

Making friends is as easy as going up to a stranger and greeting them, but creating friendships that last takes work. Have the confidence to build connections with people and the patience to nurture them into lasting friendships. Sometimes those friendships won't work out, but that's okay. As we grow, we learn, and there are lessons you can take out of every experience, even the negative ones. Remember that not everyone will like you, and that's okay. What's important is that you like yourself, and the only way to do that is to be authentic and assertive. Remember that your vibe attracts your tribe, so be the kind of person you'd want to hang around with!

When it comes to school, focus on your mission, avoid unnecessary conflicts, and learn to manage your time effectively. School is about so much more than just books, and learning doesn't only happen in the classroom. So many of the skills you'll need to know to become successful someday are things you'll learn from the way you interact with your peers at school. Leadership isn't a title; it's a state of mind. That means you don't need to be elected class president to see yourself as someone who can motivate and inspire those around you. Surround yourself with inspiring people and make sure they align with where you see yourself going. Avoiding conflict isn't always possible, so you should learn how to handle it effectively. Sometimes, the best thing you can do is to just walk away. If walking away isn't an option (for example, if you're being bullied), don't be too afraid to reach out and ask for help.

Taking care of yourself is an important part of growing up. Knowing how to cook for yourself, keeping yourself clean, and keeping yourself healthy are all very important things you need to learn if you ever plan on living on your own. Cooking skills can make the difference between a balanced diet and constant takeout; remember, a healthy body makes a healthy mind. Sticking to a routine—including personal hygiene—will help you stay on top of any changes that you might be dealing with. Change is a part of life, and it happens to all of us, but that doesn't mean it isn't scary. It's okay to be confused and wonder what's going on, so don't be afraid to reach out to someone you can trust and ask for support.

Personal development is more like running a long race, not a quick sprint. You're gonna be growing and developing for the rest of your life, so make the most of it! Keep growing, learning, and motivating yourself to be better. Through this journey, you've unearthed so many new things about yourself and discovered things that you never knew. Don't forget those things; use them as the foundation of the person you're going to become. Now that you've discovered the super you, never forget who you are!

Ultimately, becoming successful is about nurturing the right skills when you're young and perfecting them as you grow older. Success is a lifestyle that involves every aspect of your life. You need to put work into becoming the person you want to be; it doesn't just happen by luck or accident. You can do that by setting yourself goals and holding yourself accountable for achieving them. Looking after your health, wellness, and money is crucial. Make sure that you buy things that are really worth their cost and learn how to save your money. You'll thank yourself later!

Most importantly, enjoy the ride. Yeah, there's a lot to do and so much pressure to achieve, but you're only young once. Try not to take yourself too seriously. Life is meant to be enjoyed, so make sure that you do!

I hope we cross paths in the future, maybe at a different stage of your life, but until that happens, know that I'll always be rooting for you. See you later, pal!

Leave us a Review!

Hey there! Now that you've got all the cool tools to rock at life. How about helping others do the same? Just drop your honest review about this book on Amazon.

You'll help other kids find this awesome guide and kickstart their own adventure in growing up. Thanks a bunch for helping out. By sharing what you know, you're part of a super team spreading good vibes and smart tips. Your review really matters in this big mission.

Scan the QR code or visit the link. Thank you! (https://www.amazon.com/review/review-your-purch ases/?asin=B0D6BFRRL7).

REFERENCES

Anthony, M. (2019). *The social and emotional lives of 8- to 10-year-olds.* Scholastic. https://www.scholastic.com/parents/family-life/social-emotional-learning/development-milestones/emotional-lives-8-10-year-olds.html

ashley. (2024, January 5). *Creating a vision board for teens | Atlanta teen photographer.* Urban Trend Studios. https://urbantrendstudios.com/vision-board-for-atlanta-teens/

Author, N. O. M. G. (2023, June 15). *Helping your tweens & teens build healthy friendships.* New Orleans Mom. https://neworleansmom.com/ages-stages/teenagers/helping-your-tweens-teens-build-healthy-friendships/

Barney, N. (2023, March). *Leadership.* TechTarget. https://www.techtarget.com/searchcio/definition/leadership#:~:text=Leader

Beecher, H. W. (n.d.). *The body is like a piano, and happiness is like music. It is needful to have the instrument in good order.* My Best Self 101.

Berg, M. H. (2019, April 30). *How to teach resilience: The secret weapon of strong kids.* Your Teen Media. https://yourteenmag.com/health/teenager-mental-health/how-to-teach-resilience

Bradberry, T. & Greaves, J. (2009). *Emotional intelligence 2.0.* TalentSmart.

Breitegan, J. (n.d.). *Colonel Sanders: Rejected 1,009 times before starting KFC.* Learning Elephant. https://www.elephantlearning.com/post/colonel-sanders-rejected-over-one-thousand-times-before-starting-kfc

Brian, P. (2021, September 26). *25 resilient people who overcame failure to achieve huge success.* Ideapod. https://ideapod.com/resilient-people-who-overcame-failure-to-achieve-huge-success/

Brigden, B. (2022, September 29). *Leadership and teamwork: 10 ways leaders can help their teams.* Teamwork.com. https://www.teamwork.com/blog/10-ways-leaders-teams/

Britton, R. (2022, December 20). *5 basic first aid skills for kids.* Simple Family Preparedness. https://simplefamilypreparedness.com/essential-child-first-aid-skills/

Brouhard, R. (2021, November 3). *8 safety and first aid tips for kids.* Verywell Health. https://www.verywellhealth.com/safety-tips-for-kids-1298395

Buffett, W. (n.d.). *Do not save what is left after spending, but spend what is left after saving.* Goodreads.

Butterworth, E. (n.d.). *Don't go through life, grow through life.* Goodreads.

Cherry, K. (2022, October 6). *10 ways to build resilience.* Verywell Mind. https://www.verywellmind.com/ways-to-become-more-resilient-2795063

Claiborne, C. (1983). *Craig Claiborne's A feast made for laughter.* Henry & Holt Co.

Communication, C. P. T. (2022, September 4). *Ways for teens to tackle problems.* Center for Parent & Teen Communication. https://parentandteen.com/stress-management-for-teens-identify-and-then-tackle-the-problem/

Cullins, A. (2019, March 30). *9 activities to build grit and resilience in children.* Big Life Journal. https://biglifejournal.com/blogs/blog/activities-grit-resilience-children

Else. (2023, December 6). *Navigating life's obstacles: A guide for teens and young adults.* Emergent Life Skills and Education Consulting. https://emergentlifeskills.com/navigating-lifes-obstacles-a-guide-for-teens-and-young-adults/

First aid facts for kids. (2023, October 16). Kiddle Encyclopedia. https://kids.kiddle.co/First_aid#First_Aid_Kits

5 facts about goal setting. (2024, January). Nemours TeensHealth. https://kidshealth.org/en/teens/goals-tips.html

Fleming, W. (2023, June 21). *10 common problems middle school girls face (and how parents can help).* Parenting Teens and Tweens. https://parentingteensandtweens.com/10-common-problems-middle-school-girls-face/

Ford, G. R. (n.d.). *Nothing in life is more important than the ability to communicate effectively.* Goodreads.

Francis, M. (n.d.). *Cleaning and organizing is a practice, not a project.* The Gone App.

Garey, J. (2023, October 30). *Parenting tweens: What you should know.* Child Mind Institute. https://childmind.org/article/what-parents-should-know-about-tweens/

Goff, S. (2019, September 23). *Friendship factor: Making and keeping friends.* Focus on the Family. https://www.focusonthefamily.com/parenting/friendship-factor-making-and-keeping-friends/

Gough, E., Jr. (2021, May 28). *How to help your teen overcome challenges.* Dad Central. https://dadcentral.ca/how-to-help-your-teen-overcome-challenges/

Greenhalgh, A. (2020, December 14). *Teaching basic first aid to kids.* Run Wild My Child. https://runwildmychild.com/teaching-first-aid/

Horn, M. (2022, June 22). *Who can I talk to at the school?* Spark Their Future. https://www.sparktheirfuture.qld.edu.au/who-can-i-talk-to-at-the-school/

How do play & leisure contribute to children's development?. (2022, September 5). Play Like Mum. https://www.playlikemum.com/how-play-leisure-contribute-to-childrens-development/#:~:text=In%20particular%2C%20make%2Dbelieve%20play

How parents can support emotional regulation for kids and teens. (2022, January 17). Newport Academy. https://www.newportacademy.com/resources/empowering-teens/emotional-regulation-for-kids/

How to build healthy digital habits: 5 tips for families. (2023, November 14). American Academy of Pediatrics. https://www.healthychildren.org/English/family-life/Media/Pages/how-to-build-healthy-digital-habits-tips-for-families.aspx#:~:text=Balance%20family%20time%20%26%20screen%20time&text=Set%20do%2Dnot%2Ddisturb%20times

Hurley, K. (2022, July 14). *What is resilience? Your guide to facing life's challenges, adversities, and crises.* Everyday Health. https://www.everydayhealth.com/wellness/resilience/

Iannelli, V. (2022, June 23). *How kids make and keep friends.* Verywell Family. https://www.verywellfamily.com/making-and-keeping-friends-2633627

The importance of goal-setting for teens. (2022, January 19). Boys & Girls Clubs of America. https://www.bgca.org/news-stories/2022/January/the-importance-of-goal-setting-for-teens#:~:text=Teenage%20goal%2Dsetting%20can%20help

Jacobs, R. (2014, August 26). *Teaching my child first aid: 6 essentials*. Eartheasy. https://learn.eartheasy.com/articles/teaching-my-child-first-aid-6-essentials/

Jong, J. D. (2022, May 18). *How to cultivate teen leadership*. Camp Genesis. https://campgenesis.co.za/how-to-cultivate-teen-leadership/

kirrileet. (2020, June 19). *How to make a vision board*. Teen Breathe. https://teenbreathe.com.au/activities/how-to-make-a-vision-board/

Kristenson, S. (2023, September 3). 21 *self-awareness activities for kids & young students*. Happier Human. https://www.happierhuman.com/self-awareness-activities-kids/

Lake, C. (2023, October 25). *Developing teen leadership*. The Youth Excellence Society. https://www.theyes.ca/post/developing-teen-leadership

Makvana, H. (2023, August 18). 7 *useful tips to help your teens solve their problems*. MomJunction. https://www.momjunction.com/articles/help-your-teen-solve-her-problems_00326769/

Mandela, N. (1998). *The greatest glory in living lies not in never falling, but in rising every time we fall*. Forbes.

Martin, A. (2023, November 10). Coping with change: Teaching adaptability will help kids grow. *The Conversation*. https://theconversation.com/coping-with-change-teaching-adaptability-will-help-kids-grow-19726

Maxwell, J. C. (n.d.). *A leader is one who knows the way, goes the way, and shows the way*. Goodreads.

McCrohan, L. (2018, March 26). *Empower our teens to be compassionate leaders*. The Gottman Institute. https://www.gottman.com/blog/empower-teens-compassionate-leaders/

Meier, J. D. (n.d.). *What is a mindset?* Sources of Insight. https://sourcesofinsight.com/what-is-mindset/middleearthnj. (2019, June 17). *Raise a teen who can adapt to change*. Middle Earth. https://middleearthnj.org/2019/06/17/raise-a-teen-who-can-adapt-to-change/

Miller, D. (2018, February 27). *Enough. It's time to stop using the "mean girl" label for teenagers*. Women's Agenda. https://womensagenda.com.au/leadership/advice/steps-help-teen-girls-resolve-conflict/

Miranda. (2017, April 17). 6 *activities to help teens discover their passion and purpose*. The Reluctant Cowgirl. https://thereluctantcowgirl.com/help-teens-discover-passion/

Motivation and the power of not giving up. (2024, January). Nemours TeensHealth. https://kidshealth.org/en/teens/motivation.html

Muriel, C. (2022, May 8). 20 *fun conflict resolution activities for kids (printable PDF): Worksheets, games and activities*. Very Special Tales. https://veryspecialtales.com/conflict-resolution-activities-for-kids-pdf/

Perry, E. (2022a, July 22). 18 *leadership qualities and characteristics of a successful leader*. BetterUp. https://www.betterup.com/blog/leadership-characteristics

Perry, E. (2022b, September 14). *What is self-awareness and how to develop it*. BetterUp. https://www.betterup.com/blog/what-is-self-awareness

Pontz, E. (2018, September 4). *The importance of mentors for teens*. Center for Parent & Teen Communication. https://parentandteen.com/importance-adult-mentors/

Price-Mitchell, M. (2011, June 26). *What teens learn by overcoming challenges*. Psychology Today. https://www.psychologytoday.com/intl/blog/the-moment-youth/201106/what-teens-learn-overcoming-challenges

Problem solving and teenagers. (n.d.). ReachOut. https://parents.au.reachout.com/skills-to-build/connecting-and-communicating/problem-solving-and-teenagers

Problem-solving steps: Pre-teens and teenagers. (2021, November 11). raisingchildrenlnet.au. ren Network. https://raisingchildren.net.au/pre-teens/behaviour/encouraging-good-behaviour/problem-solving-steps

Raypole, C. (2020, August 27). *8 ways to truly enjoy the little things*. Healthline. https://www.healthline.com/health/enjoy-the-little-things#takeaway

Resilience. (n.d.). American Psychological Association. https://www.apa.org/topics/resilience#~:text=Resilience%20is%20the%20process%20and

Resilience for teens: 10 tips to build skills on bouncing back from rough times. (2020). American Psychological Association. https://www.apa.org/topics/resilience/bounce-teens

Reynolds, N. (2020, May 26). *Raising Leaders: 8 tips to teach your teen to be a leader, not a follower*. Raising Teens Today. https://raisingteenstoday.com/raising-leaders-teach-your-teen-how-to-lead/

Rohn, J. (n.d.). *Take care of your body, it's the only place you have to live*. BrainyQuote.

The role of play in the mental health of children. (2021, February 17). Miracle Recreation. https://www.miracle-recreation.com/blog/role-of-play-in-the-children-mental-health/?lang=can

Roosevelt, E. (n.d.). *The future belongs to those who believe in the beauty of their dreams*. Goodreads.

Russell, L. (2023, June 14). *Helping your child cope with setbacks*. They Are the Future. https://www.theyarethefuture.co.uk/helping-child-cope-setbacks/

Sabrina. (2020, April 15). *7 simple tips to help you enjoy the little things in life*. The Budding Optimist. https://buddingoptimist.com/enjoy-the-little-things

Schwarz, N. (2017, September 6). *How to teach growth mindset to teens*. Big Life Journal. https://biglifejournal.com/blogs/blog/teaching-teens-growth-mindset

Shaw, G. B. (n.d.). *We don't stop playing because we grow old; we grow old because we stop playing*. Goodreads.

Sherman, B. (n.d.). *Take some time to learn first aid and CPR. It saves lives, and it works*. BrainyQuote.

6 secrets to becoming an inspiring teen leader!. (2024). We Think Twice. https://www.wethinktwice.acf.hhs.gov/6-secrets-becoming-inspiring-teen-leader#~:text=Be%20a%20role%20model.

Sleep in middle and high school students. (2020, September 10). Centers for Disease Control and Prevention. https://www.cdc.gov/healthyschools/features/students-sleep.htm#print

Staff, A. (2022, September 29). *8 tips to help kids establish healthy habits around the devices in your home*. Amazon. https://www.aboutamazon.com/news/devices/8-tips-to-help-kids-establish-healthy-habits-around-the-devices-in-your-home

Staff, L. E. (2023, December 1). *12 characteristics of a good leader*. Center for Creative Leadership. https://www.ccl.org/articles/leading-effectively-articles/characteristics-good-leader/#~:text=A%20good%20leader%20should%20have

Staff, M. C. (2023, July 27). *Cardiopulmonary resuscitation: CPR. First aid*. Mayo Clinic. https://www.mayoclinic.org/first-aid/first-aid-cpr/basics/art-20056600

Starikova, A. (2021, November 3). *Seven digital habits for today's children*. Kaspersky Daily. https://www.kaspersky.com/blog/top-digital-habits-2021/42793/

The story of IKEA. (n.d.). IKEA. https://www.ikea.com/global/en/our-business/how-we-work/story-of-ikea/

Team, C. (2023, March 23). *How to put together a first aid kit for children: A first aid kit checklist*. Cleanipedia. https://www.cleanipedia.com/za/family/how-to-put-together-a-first-aid-kit-for-children-a-first-aid-kit-checklist.html

interObservers. (2023, May 23). *10 leadership activities for teens: Empower the leaders of tomorrow*. interObservers. https://interobservers.com/leadership-activities-for-teens/

pathway2success. (2021, October 18). *10+ self-awareness activities for kids*. The Pathway 2 Success. https://www.thepathway2success.com/10-self-awareness-activities-for-kids/

Tips to help your teen cultivate their passion. (2019, December 31). Raising Healthy Teens. https://raisinghealthyteens.org/tips-to-help-your-teen-cultivate-their-passion/

Underwood, K. (2023, May 7). *The power of mindset and how to leverage it for success.* Clever Girl Finance. https://www.clevergirlfinance.com/power-of-mindset/#:~:text=Mindsets%20can%20play%20a%20big

Vaughan-Smith, H. (2022, November 19). *Goal-setting for teens The SMART way to success (parent guide).* They Are the Future. https://www.theyarethefuture.co.uk/smart-goals-teens/

Veitch, J. (2016). *The agony of trying to unsubscribe.* TEDSummit. https://www.ted.com/talks/james_veitch_the_agony_of_trying_to_unsubscribe

What defines young leaders? More research could benefit youth and society broadly. (2022, November 15). Association for Psychological Science. https://www.psychologicalscience.org/news/2022-november-adolescent-leadership.html

Williams, A. (2021, October 15). *The impact of having a good mentor.* First Tee. https://firsttee.org/2021/10/15/the-impact-of-having-a-good-mentor/?gad_source=1&gclid=CjwKCAiA1MCrBhAoEiwAC2d64WqQRC3gfgurWYsTYY6r3p4dUy2Ch3XY_ubQwsPtqWK4opwLAv7iEBoCrooQAvD_BwE

Wilson, W. (1856). *Friendship is the only cement that will ever hold the world together.* Goodreads.

Wise, T. & Smarts, M. (2018). *Helping our kids navigate a digital world.* Media Smarts. https://mediasmarts.ca/sites/default/files/guides/guide_helping_kids_navigate_digital_world.pdf

X, M. (1964, June 28). *Education is the passport to the future, for tomorrow belongs to those who prepare for it today.* Address on behalf of the Organization of Afro-American Unity (OAAU). https://www.blackpast.org/african-american-history/speeches-african-american-history/1964-malcolm-x-s-speech-founding-rally-organization-afro-american-unity/

Zapata, K. (2020, September 28). *The importance of play: How kids learn by having fun.* Healthline. https://www.healthline.com/health/the-importance-of-play